RETENTION AND RESISTANCE

RETENTION AND RESISTANCE

Writing Instruction and Students Who Leave

PEGEEN REICHERT POWELL

UTAH STATE UNIVERSITY PRESS
Logan

Published by Utah State University Press
An imprint of University Press of Colorado
5589 Arapahoe Avenue, Suite 206C
Boulder, Colorado 80303

 The University Press of Colorado is a proud member of
the Association of American University Presses.

The University Press of Colorado is a cooperative publishing enterprise supported, in part, by Adams State University, Colorado State University, Fort Lewis College, Metropolitan State University of Denver, Regis University, University of Colorado, University of Northern Colorado, Utah State University, and Western State Colorado University.

Cover design by Dan Miller

∞ The paper used in this publication meets the minimum requirements of the American National Standard for Information Sciences – Permanence of Paper for Printed Library Materials. ANSI Z39.48-1992

A previous version of chapter 1 appeared originally as "Retention Risks and Realities: One Student's Story," coauthored with Danielle Aquiline, in *Open Words: Access and English Studies* 3, no. 2 (Fall 2009). Parts of the introduction and chapter 1 appeared originally as "Retention and Writing Instruction: Implications for Access and Pedagogy," in *College Composition and Communication* 60, no. 4 (June 2009).

ISBN: 978-0-87421-930-2 (paperback)
ISBN: 978-0-87421-931-9 (ebook)

Cataloging information for this title is available at the Library of Congress.
Cover image © xamnediacx/Shutterstock

For J.V., J.O., and A.F.

CONTENTS

ACKNOWLEDGMENTS

The early stages of research for this book were supported by the Multicultural Enrichment Grant Program at Columbia College Chicago. A grant from that program enabled me to create, with Kilian McCurrie, the Student Faculty Partnership for Success program, which partnered faculty members for one year with students who were at risk for leaving college before graduation. Those faculty, Kilian, Amanda Johnson, and Danielle Aquiline devoted hours to supporting and mentoring their students. Danielle deserves special thanks here, not only for her participation in that program, but for her collaboration on an early version of chapter 1, which appeared in *Open Words: Access and English Studies* (Fall 2009), and for the many conversations about how to support students who might leave. I also want to acknowledge all of the Columbia College students who participated in the program, who gave us their time and trust.

Any reader of this book will appreciate that it simply would not have been possible without the participation of the three students whose stories I tell. I marvel at their persistence and intelligence; their effort to stay in touch, even now that the research is completed, humbles me. I hope to honor their ongoing stories not just with this book but with every class I teach from now on.

I would also like to thank Joe Harris and Michael Spooner, who supported this book at crucial points in the process. Joe's comments on an early draft, and those of the reviewers he solicited, shaped the book in significant ways. Earlier versions of portions of the introduction and chapter 1 appeared in *College Composition and Communication* (June 2009).

I am also very grateful to my parents, who provided me respite from my other responsibilities when I needed to concentrate on writing and some of the most sincere cheers when I experienced moments of success. As I write this page, Charlie is at yet another karate tournament, modeling a determination and work ethic I aspire to, and Elizabeth is lying on the floor playing the harmonica, embodying joys and talents I will likely never experience. They inspire me every day. And there is really no sufficient way to thank Doug, except to list him last.

RETENTION AND RESISTANCE

INTRODUCTION

Paying Attention to the Discourse
of Retention in Higher Education

> *It is from the idea that we can and should*
> *succeed that failure is born.*
> —David Payne 1989, *Coping with*
> *Failure: The Therapeutic Uses of Rhetoric*

> *[College] was a major step, and it was something that I need-*
> *ed because God knows, if I didn't have a taste of what college*
> *was like, I might still be on the streets because I wouldn't*
> *know where to go back to now.*
> —Helen[1]

In the fall of 2008, my two sections of first-year writing were positively electric with the excitement of the campaign and ultimately the election of Barack Obama. I had designed the course to tap into that fall's election, and I enjoyed teaching these two particularly motivated, bright, cohesive groups of students. Two years later, in fall 2010, only eight of the twenty-four students from those classes were still enrolled at my institution. Our institution-wide retention rate for their cohort two years later was 52 percent, and our current graduation rate is 41 percent; neither are rates my college is satisfied with, but they are better than the distressing 33 percent retention rate among the students in my two classes (Columbia College Chicago 2013).

In his first address to the joint session of congress in February 2009, President Obama identified college retention as one of the major initiatives of his administration: "In a global economy where the most valuable skill you can sell is your knowledge, a good education is no longer just a pathway to opportunity—it is a pre-requisite. . . . That is why we will provide the support necessary for you to complete college and meet a new goal: by 2020, America will once again have the

DOI: 10.7330/9780874219319.c000

highest proportion of college graduates in the world" (Obama 2009a). And a few months later, he announced the American Graduation Initiative, with the goal that the United States will regain its place as the country with the highest proportion of college graduates (Obama 2009c).

Even before President Obama announced his education agenda, the powerful College Board established the Commission on Access, Admissions and Success in Higher Education, which created the College Completion Agenda. Among other efforts, the Agenda identifies criteria and makes recommendations for improving state policy and has set a goal that 55 percent of all twenty-five- to thirty-four-year-olds will hold an associate degree or higher by 2025 (College Board 2011). Around the same time, the equally powerful Gates Foundation identified college graduation as one of its top concerns, launching Complete College America, the central feature of which is the Alliance of States (currently there are twenty-nine) involving states that have committed to identifying and implementing state-level policies that will improve the graduation rate nationally and collecting data to measure progress (Complete College America 2011).

But the discourse of retention is not just circulating among national-level policy wonks. This discourse is circulating within higher education as well. Increasingly, graduation rates have become a key factor in students' decisions about enrolling in a college or university. These rates have been available for a while, ever since it became mandatory that institutions post them as part of the Student Right-to-Know Act, but they have become easier for students and their families, as responsible consumers, to find; for example, on the Integrated Postsecondary Education Data System, or IPEDS, students can compare colleges or universities across several variables, including graduation and loan default rates (IPEDS 2013). More recently, in winter 2013, the White House launched the College Scorecard, which enables students' families to search in a variety of ways for data on specific institutions, and which features most prominently the institution's costs and graduation rates (White House 2013). This scrutiny on the part of students and their families is, understandably, compelling colleges and universities to pay more attention than ever before to retention.

The term *retention* in higher education refers to the ability of an institution to keep students enrolled until graduation, and the federal government maintains standards and definitions for calculating and reporting institutions' ability to do so. (The Integrated Postsecondary Education Data System is a reliable source for such standards and definitions; see IPEDS 2013.) However, in current discourse, retention also signifies more generally the problem of students leaving college before graduation, the tremendous efforts of colleges and universities to prevent this from happening, the rapidly growing body of research and scholarship that surrounds the problem, and, increasingly, the for-profit consulting enterprises that sell solutions. This discourse also entails significant questions about whether higher education is a right or a privilege, about an institution's or an instructor's responsibility to individual students, about what and how we teach when we know students may leave. It is this larger, admittedly messier, discourse, and especially the ways this discourse intersects with my work as a writing teacher, that I am concerned with in this book.

It is easy to believe we're hearing more about retention recently because of the economy. For example, President Obama set his agenda during an international financial collapse, and the merit of promoting more college graduates at that time seemed obvious. More locally, likewise, we might blame the economy for the drone of this buzzword at our own institutions. A dominant feature of the discourse of retention is the idea that college is an investment (my own college president used this very term at a recent graduation), but the difficulty of securing loans and grants makes families much more cautious about where and how they invest their money. At my institution, we hear that, in this current economy, families do not see a private arts and media college education as a wise investment. Therefore, we need to work harder to keep the students we already have: retention.

This is a "Why-Johnny-Can't-Read" moment, when popular and political discourses intersect with our work in the classroom in significant, material ways. And for those of us whose careers are devoted to college-level teaching, this kind of pervasive attention to the importance of helping students graduate from college is very seductive. As instructors, the discourse of retention appeals to our benevolence and our self-interest at the same time. Almost every teacher I know has a story about that one bright, engaged student, and most of us have several stories, several students who just disappeared. Sometimes they leave in the middle of the semester, no good-byes, no explanations. Sometimes they come to us after handing in the final project, and with head down, in deflated tones, admit they won't be back next semester. "Money problems," they say, or "the family situation, y'know." Sometimes we might have predicted they would leave, but, for me at least, expecting this outcome makes it worse: I wanted this one to beat the odds. At the same time, the discourse of retention also appeals to our self-interest: at my institution, it is declining enrollment and retention rates that explain why full-time faculty don't get the cost-of-living raise this year and why part-time faculty lost sections at the last minute. We come to understand that butts in seats mean money in pockets. It's a seductive discourse.

I admit: I was seduced. This project is motivated by my experiences in the writing class, classes like those I taught in fall 2008, when the energy of the semester inevitably yielded to the disappointment as one student, then another, then yet others, left. As a faculty member concerned about the financial health of my place of employment, I pay attention to our graduation rates and efforts to improve them. However, as a teacher of first-year writing and a composition studies scholar, I undertook this project primarily because I became frustrated as I watched my students leave. I found myself reading retention scholarship, assuming there must be something I could learn that would increase their chances of sticking around. I received a grant from my institution's Office of Multicultural Affairs to establish a one-year program to work closely with a group of students whose profile suggested they were at risk for dropping out. I figured I'd learn from students what the "real" issues were. I read more retention scholarship (chapter 1 provides a brief survey of retention scholarship).

This book is the result of my immersion in the discourse of retention. Or more accurately, it is the result of my critical engagement with this discourse as it circulates at my institution and elsewhere and my increasing skepticism about the utility of the growing body of scholarship on retention, or at least its applicability to my work as a writing teacher. Retention tends to function metonymically in higher education today. Metonymy is one of Kenneth Burke's four "master tropes"; Burke explains, "The basic 'strategy' in metonymy is this: to convey some incorporeal or intangible state in terms of the corporeal or tangible" (Burke 1969, 506). Metonymy, according to Burke, is fundamentally, a strategy of reduction (507). In this case, retention functions metonymically by reducing a variety of intangibles—student success and failure, the value of higher education in general, the purpose of courses like first-year writing in particular, and so on—to a set of tangible numbers, or even to something more corporeal: butts in seats. The difference between metaphor and metonymy is that while metaphor works by putting two different cognitive frames together, metonymy works with both the target and the vehicle operating in the same cognitive frame (Feyaerts and Brone 2005, 14). Robert Frost famously argues that "all metaphor breaks down somewhere"; despite the important difference between metaphor and metonymy, I would extend Frost's assertion to metonymy (Frost 2007, 107). At some point, we simply can't reduce student success and failure, the value of higher education, or the purpose of our courses, to a set of numbers. Retention, as a figure of speech, breaks down. My project here can be understood as seeking out those breaking points, exploiting them, and not only critiquing the potential damage this figure can wreak but also reversing the reduction and identifying some of the real issues hidden therein.

Throughout the book, I explore the discourse of retention and present a twofold argument. On one hand, I argue that faculty must be mindful as this discourse circulates in our institutions. We must be attentive to the material and conceptual implications of this discourse as it affects our curricula and job descriptions and also as it circumscribes our understanding of "the student" and the purpose of higher education. On the other hand, however, I argue that the discourse of retention holds heuristic value for everyone in higher education: when students drop out, we confront our own limits as educators. How can we achieve our pedagogical goals or institutional missions when students leave? How might we reframe the discourse of retention so it is as much about educating the students in front of us as it is about trying to keep students here?

A note about vocabulary: *retention* refers to the rate at which institutions keep students until they graduate; *persistence* refers to an individual student's decision and effort to graduate, regardless of the institution. Persistence rates, therefore, track a student who transfers to various institutions. I will refer to *retention* throughout the book unless I intend to make this distinction because *retention* is the common label for the complex of problems I am discussing. However, I believe our goal should not be to improve retention rates but to help each student who is willing and able to persist (see Hagedorn 2005, 92, for a discussion of these terms).

PAYING ATTENTION

Because retention is such a complicated and important problem, it is understandable that some scholars, politicians, and higher-education administrators forget that, in Jennifer L. Crissman Ishler and M. Lee Upcraft's words, "Retention should never be the goal of an institution" (Ishler and Upcraft 2005, 45). Rather, student learning, or education more broadly, should always be the primary motivation. Moreover, Upcraft, John N. Gardner, and Betsy O. Barefoot recognize that "retention as a linchpin for successful first-year initiatives will never be successful in engaging sufficient numbers of educators, particularly faculty. Faculty see themselves as dedicated to student learning in their classrooms, not to keeping students in college, and they are absolutely correct in this belief" (Upcraft, Gardener, and Barefoot

2005, 6). Their statement here provides one of the reasons, I argue, that faculty should pay attention to retention efforts at their respective institutions: faculty can provide an important check to ensure that we retain a focus on teaching and learning rather than on simply keeping students in seats.

And faculty who regularly teach first-year students, such as writing instructors, should especially pay attention to the discourse about retention at their respective institutions because a fairly common assumption in retention scholarship is that efforts should be focused on first-year students. As Upcraft, Gardner, and Barefoot claim, there is "overwhelming evidence that student success is largely determined by student experiences during the first year" (Upcraft, Gardener, and Barefoot 2005, 1). Attrition rates for students between their first and second years are the highest of all four years, and these attrition rates are a fairly strong indicator of the institution's overall graduation rates; therefore, presumably, efforts aimed at improving retention after the first year will have a positive ripple effect on rates in subsequent years (Levitz, Noel, and Richter 1999, 36).

The focus on the first year has to do with the nature of many students' transition into higher education: Randi S. Levitz, Lee Noel, and Beth J. Richter argue that "freshman need a prevention plan. Intrusive, proactive strategies must be used to reach freshman before the students have an opportunity to experience feelings of failure, disappointment, and confusion" (Levitz, Noel, and Richter 1999, 39; cf. Tinto 1987, 58). "Intrusive" strategies advocated by scholars of the first-year experience include radically redesigning orientation, developmental studies, advising, and residential-life programs; more fully integrating academics and student life through programs like living-learning communities; and requiring a first-year seminar of all students (see Kuh 2005, 99–107). It should be clear by scanning this list just how writing faculty could choose to or be required to participate in these retention efforts. Just in the last few years, at two different institutions, I have witnessed a first-year advising program that expected faculty to facilitate students' social as well as academic integration into college;

the removal of a writing center from the authority of English department faculty and into a more general academic support center; a living-learning program instituted without input from writing faculty, even though the writing course was one of the key features of the program; and first-year seminars whose goals and methods sometimes overlap those of the first-year writing class—all of these in the name of retention.

The unique context of the writing classroom as an interface between students' past and future educational experiences, as an introduction to the discourse practices of higher education, and as one of the only universal requirements at most institutions, makes it a prime site for retention efforts. However, the focus on the first year in retention literature does not always translate to a focus on pedagogy or to a reliance on the expertise of faculty who regularly teach first-year students. Retention research has not circulated among scholars in traditional academic disciplines but among individuals whose training and careers have been located primarily in administration. Moreover, some institutional conditions—for example, the persistent division between student affairs and academic affairs— perpetuate the disconnect between conversations about retention and conversations about pedagogy. As retention efforts move into classrooms, writing programs must be informed about the politics and priorities of retention efforts at our respective institutions so composition faculty are not recruited to participate in efforts that run counter to our own goals and pedagogies. For example, the first-year seminar touted as a successful retention effort could either replace first-year writing altogether at some institutions or be added to the course load of writing faculty who are familiar with the kind of teaching required by these seminars: discussion-dominated classes heavy on writing and often based in the humanities. These changes to the first-year curriculum are not necessarily negative, but they are worthy of careful consideration and plenty of campus-wide conversation. Moreover, composition faculty would bring particular attitudes, experiences, and knowledge to such conversations about retention: namely, we have a disciplinary history of institutional critique and discourse analysis that would provide an important context and a healthy skepticism about retention efforts; we know first-year students well simply because we see so many of them in the intimate settings of the writing classroom and student conferences; and we have a commitment to pedagogy that most of us would be unwilling to compromise in the name of keeping tuition dollars in the institution.

I also assert that there is value to our own work as teachers and scholars of writing in thinking carefully about the issues that circulate around the problem of retention. Specifically, the problem of retention in higher education—of students who leave and our efforts to keep them enrolled—can help reframe questions about the viability and purpose of the universal requirement of first-year writing, questions that persist at the center of the history and identity of composition studies. Richard Miller, in an opinion piece titled "Our Future Donors," argues that compositionists should begin to see "students as future donors" in order to advocate for first-year writing. He explains that "the case can be made that it is now crucial to the long-term financial well-being of public institutions of higher education to improve the working conditions of writing instructors, precisely because writing programs have access to all those impressionable and invaluable future donors" (R. Miller 2004, 378). He is able to make this argument in part because the results of retention research suggest just how important the first year is to keeping students satisfied and enrolled, creating happy and, hopefully, generous alumni. In other words, improved status for first-year writing—which, among other benefits, would reduce class sizes and entice full-time professors to commit to the intellectual project (or so the argument goes), and thus to a higher-quality educational experience—will in turn lead to improved retention rates.

His argument is frustratingly circular: composition studies professionals should represent the first-year students they teach as future donors so that composition studies professionals are in a position to continue teaching first-year students/future donors. But why do we want to continue teaching first-year students, and if we can answer that question, then what should we be teaching them? Few scholars in composition studies dispute the fact that "the first-year course which was our beginning has maintained its position at the center of our enterprise" (Roemer, Schultz, and Durst 1999, 377). Even strong abolitionist arguments, such as Sharon Crowley's, concede that "composition instruction is firmly associated with the curriculum of the required introductory course or courses in composition" (Crowley 1995). What is disputed is the question of why we, as a discipline, require the first-year course and define our work as much as we do in terms of its curriculum.

The debate about the universal requirement is often reduced to a debate about disciplinarity and composition's status and role in the institution. As Marjorie Roemer, Lucille M. Schultz, and Russel K. Durst explain, "The impetus to separate composition as a field from the complicated position of the required first-year writing course has been in part a desire to escape the demoted status associated with courses that are introductory, mandated, viewed as 'remedial,' and labeled under the heading of 'service'" (Roemer, Schultz, and Durst 1999, 389). Some, like Roemer, Schultz, and Durst, argue, however, that "service," while once a "term of denigration," is now "making a comeback as a term that garners support for socially responsible action connecting the university with its larger environment" (387). Jeff Smith agrees and argues that, even apart from any sense of social action, he understands his role "as contained within, and constrained by, the university's overall curriculum," and that's okay: "I want my efforts to converge, in the end, with the university's . . . I am willing, in that sense, to try to make what I teach *useful*" (Smith 1997, 318–19). Sharon Crowley, on the other hand, argues that if "the required introductory course remains in place in order to socialize students into the discourse of the academy, to the extent that it succeeds in this it supplements or even erases students' home languages" (Crowley 1995). Crowley's arguments raise questions about the ideological implications of first-year composition, arguments that by now are familiar to most composition studies scholars and teachers. She concludes that we should distinguish composition from writing because the former is "saturated with the discourse of formal correctness" and then "abandon the service ethic of remediation" in favor of "the study, practice, and teaching of writing" (Crowley 1995).

I believe arguments like Crowley's are so powerful and yet so anxiously dismissed in professional conversations because their occasional appearance reminds us that the purpose and significance of our work are not necessarily self-evident. However, even if they were self-evident, knowing that, depending on where we teach, up to 50 percent of our students in first-year writing will never graduate, and that possibly up to 30 percent won't even stick around for sophomore year, makes it necessary for us to completely rethink the purpose of the first-year writing course. For students who leave, the first-year course cannot operate as a service to their other courses. In chapter 4, I discuss the research on transfer, which suggests that even under the best of circumstances, students take very little with them from our writing courses into courses in other disciplines. But for the student who leaves and enrolls in another college, or takes months or years off, or who never returns, the possibility of transfer is even more drastically reduced. It is impractical (at best) to teach our course as a service to other disciplines—this simply isn't a service we can provide.

However, rather than understand this as an argument in favor of abolition, I believe the problem of attrition opens up the responsibilities and possibilities of the first-year writing course. If the majority of students who leave tend to leave after the first year, then ours is one of the few college courses they will take before they do. What should we teach them in the time they are enrolled? What about writing do we want them to experience before they leave—some headed for other colleges, some for work in service industries, some for work as caregivers, all as citizens?

No longer can we justify a course that, in Crowley's words, will "socialize students into the discourse of the academy" and erase their home languages, because we can't assume that all students, maybe not even most, are headed for years in the academy. But neither can we abandon the first-year course or focus our disciplinary energies elsewhere. How might the first-year writing course function in a context at once much broader than four consecutive years of college and as narrow as one or two semesters? If ours is one of the few courses a student might take before dropping out, or transferring to another school, or stopping out for a few semesters before returning, then what will we do with such tremendous responsibility and opportunity?

PAYING ATTENTION TO OPPORTUNITIES

The issue of attrition compels us—or allows us—to remove the first-year writing course from the imperative of chronology, from being imagined only in the context of a finite number of consecutive semesters and years. A move away from chronology begs for renewed attention to the rhetorical concept of kairos. John E. Smith explains the distinction between *chronos*, the root of *chronology*, and *kairos* this way:

> In *chronos* we have the fundamental conception of time as measure, the *quantity* of duration, the length of periodicity. . . . By contrast, the term *kairos* points to a *qualitative* character of time, to the special position an event or action occupies in a series, to a season when something appropriate happens that cannot happen just at "any time," but only at *that* time, to a time that marks an opportunity which may not recur. (John E. Smith 2002, 47)

Smith's explanation here highlights the fact that my argument, while it may require a shift in perspective, does not really require a radical change in the circumstances of teaching. *All* of our courses are *already* "a season when something appropriate happens that cannot happen just at 'any time,' but only at *that* time": a particular configuration of students in a particular space only ever happens at *that* time. What matters is that we see this as "an opportunity." It is an opportunity that will not recur for us as teachers—we will never have this roster in this space for this purpose again—and neither will such an opportunity recur for our students: while some students may go on to other courses, writing courses even, no course will present this same opportunity again. For some students who leave college never to return, the opportunity is even more rare.

A chronological pedagogy assumes a linear process, an exercise of skills development from one course to the next, as well as the curricular structures to support a predictable progression. Such a pedagogy requires that students move through the process in a certain way, but when students drop out or transfer, the process is interrupted. These interruptions are thought of as exceptions to the rule of progress. However, the issue of retention reminds us that these may not be exceptions but the rule itself in many institutions. Moreover, as I discuss in chapter 4, the research on transfer in composition studies indicates that even for students who do not leave, rarely, if ever, do skills transfer from one context to the next in the way our pedagogy and curriculum assume they will.

A kairotic pedagogy, on the other hand, is not about a linear process but about opportunities of the moment. These opportunities arise not from the place of our course in a particular sequence of events but from the particular "forces at work," to use Debra Hawhee's words: "Chronos marks duration while kairos marks force. Kairos is thus rhetoric's time, for the quality, direction, and movement of discursive encounters depend more on the forces at work on and in a particular moment than their quantifiable length" (Hawhee 2002, 18). A kairotic pedagogy does not rely on the length of time a student is enrolled, but "on the forces at work on and in the particular moment" the students are in front of us. The issue of retention reminds us of the forces in many of our students' lives that we simply have no control over: their emotional and physical health, their financial situation, their family obligations, their changing desires and goals. My frustration with retention efforts arises in part because of the hubris of trying to control these forces. A kairotic approach to teaching does not try to control these forces, ignore them, or treat them as obstacles. Hawhee argues that our discursive encounters *depend* on the forces. Thus, a kairotic pedagogy does not derive its sense of purpose from the skills a student might need later in the curriculum; a kairotic pedagogy derives its sense of purpose from the variety of forces in our classroom at any given moment, including the forces in our students' lives that may lead some of them to leave before graduation.

A renewed emphasis on kairos in pedagogy does not mean we reject chronos altogether, that we turn our backs on lesson plans and curriculum development. These exercises can provide a necessary context from which we open ourselves up to the possibilities inherent in the unique confluence of people and forces in a given space and time. Smith argues that "kairos presupposes chronos," but that chronos alone is not enough to understand those moments of "human experience where the *chronos* aspect reaches certain *critical points* at which a qualitative character begins to emerge, and when there are junctures of opportunity calling for human ingenuity in apprehending when the time is 'right'" (John E. Smith 2002, 48).

I am thinking here of teaching as a rhetorical event, comprised of written and oral performances, and the teacher as a rhetor who is capable of "ingenuity in apprehending when the time is 'right'" (John E. Smith 2002, 48). But kairos is equally useful as a key concept in the content of our courses. Despite recent reevaluations of process pedagogy, writing as process maintains a strong, unexamined hold in first-year writing courses (see Fulkerson 2005, 658). The language of brainstorming, drafts, and revision cuts across even the most divergent approaches to writing instruction, and that may be as it should be. However, equally compelling is the argument that we need to recognize those rhetorical situations our students will encounter in their lives that require more familiarity with the concept of kairos than with the practice of brainstorming. The issue of retention foregrounds the various forces in our students' lives and reminds us of the countless types of situations they will encounter when they leave our classrooms. I will return to the concept of kairos throughout the book, and particularly in chapter 4, where I focus on the implications of the issue of retention for writing pedagogy and curriculum.

PAYING ATTENTION TO ACCESS AND REMEDIATION

The issue of retention is worth paying attention to because it can help recast the old problem of the universal first-year requirement in a new light with particular implications for our pedagogy and curriculum. Retention also prompts a reconsideration of another persistent problem in composition studies: access. The history and disciplinary formation of first-year writing is inextricably tied to the problem of access. One might point to the entrance test at Harvard, instituted in 1874, as evidence: as James Berlin argues, "The test in English ensured that the new open university would not become too open" (Berlin 1987, 23). Or one might point to the role of writing instruction, and specifically the rise of basic writing, in the politics of open admissions during the 1970s (Horner and Lu 1999, 3). Tom Fox argues that "as writing teachers, we are institutionally positioned to gatekeep, to do harm. To create access, we must go against the grain" (Fox 1999, 17). The relationship between composition studies and the problem of access is complicated, but as Fox notes, the institutional position of first-year writing makes the relationship inevitable. Throughout the discourse of access as it circulates in the professional literature of composition studies, however, there is not much said about retention. Nevertheless, presumably, arguments about access are not just about getting students in the door but about providing students with an education; retention is about keeping students enrolled long enough to accomplish this goal.

Arguments in favor of increasing access to higher education that remain unqualified by the research on retention will be too simplistic to accomplish much. Historically, at the same time there have been pressures to increase access to higher education, concerns about retention rates have proliferated. In fact, the first studies of retention emerged in the 1930s at a time when enrollments were increasing, as was the value of a college degree, because of the shift to an urban industrialized society and the corresponding need for managers and professionals (Berger and Lyon 2005, 13–14). The reason for the correspondence between the issues of access and retention can be explained by the research of Alexander W. Astin; he asserts, based on his analysis of data derived from surveys of over fifty-six thousand students from across the country, that "an institution's degree completion rate is primarily a reflection of its entering student characteristics" (Astin 2005–2006, 7). I discuss Astin's claim more thoroughly in chapter 2, but for now it is worth noting what tends to be a given in retention research, that as more people from a greater variety of educational and socioeconomic backgrounds enroll in college, retention rates go down. There is a risk, in other words, that institutions could use retention data to craft admissions policies. In effect, retention could determine access. For this reason alone, the arguments that have circulated within composition studies about increasing access to higher education must address the discourse of retention.

But Astin's analysis might also help us qualify our arguments about the role of first-year writing instruction as institutional gatekeeper. The important work of scholars like Crowley, but also Victor Villanueva, Keith Gilyard, Jacqueline Jones Royster, Linda Brodkey, and Mike Rose, just to name a few, has identified the ways the language practices of the academy in general, and first-year comp in particular, are complicit in excluding those who are not white and middle class. These arguments might be more usefully reframed in terms of retention. Once students are in our classrooms, they have already, by definition, achieved access to higher education; gatekeeping is no longer the issue. What we're really talking about when we're talking about the exclusionary practices of academic discourse and the rules of Standard American English that writing teachers are expected to enforce is retention, the question of whether or not students will persist once they are in. My point here is that the discourse of retention must qualify, even radically revise, our arguments about improving access.

When we think about building or maintaining the structures necessary to help students persist, we often turn our attention to remedial education, and specifically basic writing. As the subtitle of a recent collection about this problem suggests, however, we frequently yoke basic writing to the discourse of access (see *Mainstreaming Basic Writers: Politics and Pedagogies of Access*, edited by Gerri McNenny, 2001). It is worth noting that in some colleges and universities, full access to higher education is conditional on a student's performance in basic writing, and in these cases, access and remediation obviously intersect. However, in one important essay in McNenny's collection, Mary Soliday argues that "we tend to assume that the fate of open access depends heavily upon remedial programs. In assuming such a close relationship between access and remediation, we may fix our gaze so narrowly upon the efficacy of one program that we obscure alternative explanations for students' success or failure at college" (Soliday 2001, 56).

By reframing the question of remediation in terms of retention, we get a richer, more thorough understanding of students' fate in higher education. Soliday relies on David Lavin and David Hyllegard's study of CUNY students and Marilyn Sternglass's longitudinal study of CCNY students to support her argument that remediation should be seen as only one piece of the puzzle. Lavin and Hyllegard's and Sternglass's studies both conclude that open access to higher education can improve lives. However, too closely linking access to remediation overstates the role of programs like basic writing in the students' chances for success or failure. Moreover, both studies emphasize the importance of economic factors in students' educational stories, especially as students are paying a larger portion of tuition and working part or full time to do so (Soliday 2001, 66). These studies support the findings of retention research, which indicate that money problems are a major reason for student departure. It is not just a student's inability to pay the bills that may lead to departure from college; rather, the perception that a particular college is not a worthwhile investment can compel a student to leave (Braxton and Hirschy 2005, 62).

My point here is not to dismiss the role of writing instruction, including remedial instruction, in the effort to improve access and retention, but to place that role in a larger context. In chapters 3 and 4, I draw on disability studies, as that field intersects with composition studies, to begin to theorize what it might mean to broaden the context—beyond remedial education—in order to understand and address the issues of access and retention. Disability studies scholar Jay Dolmage discusses the principles of universal design, which is meant to guide the intentional design of a physical environment that meets the needs of all people, those with disabilities and those without. Dolmage argues that these same principles can guide the building of institutional, curricular, and pedagogical structures that meet the needs of all students. In the context of retention, universal design is a useful way of imagining a way forward in higher education so that we refocus our energies not on keeping as many students as possible but on educating as many students as possible, including those who might leave before graduation.

On one hand, it is important to take seriously our responsibilities *as composition professionals* to increase the chances that students will both be admitted to college and persist once they are here. I remain committed to working toward a writing pedagogy informed by the best practices in composition studies, including those practices that remove unnecessary barriers to success. On the other hand, we can better achieve these goals if we also look at the bigger picture: and it is a very big, very complicated picture.

PAYING ATTENTION TO STUDENTS' STORIES

While I cannot claim this book will bring that picture into clearer focus, I do intend for *Retention and Resistance* to add details sometimes missing from the discourse of retention as it circulates in our institutions. A major element of my project is the stories of individual students. It was the stories of the students in my classrooms that led me to this topic in the first place, and their stories that provided an important frame against which I studied retention scholarship and my own institution's retention discourse. Specifically, informing my project is my work with a group of students from my own institution whom I came to know as part of a grant-funded program I designed called Student Faculty

Partnership for Success. This program partnered each of approximately thirty students with one of four faculty members. The faculty member contacted each student regularly throughout the academic year to check on their academic and social adjustments to college, as well as to see how they were doing physically, emotionally, financially, and so on. As the coordinator of the program, one of the faculty partners, and, in some cases, as their teacher in one or two semesters of first-year writing, I developed, and have maintained, a relationship with a few of the students, including students who have since left my institution. These students have provided me insight into the overwhelming complexities of the problem of retention and provide this project with the voices of those who are most immediately affected by our efforts—or lack thereof—to provide an education to everyone who shows up in our classrooms.

Three of these students, Helen, Cesar, and Nathan[2], have been exceptionally generous with their time and their stories. Each of chapters 1, 2, and 3 features one of their stories, set against my own research and arguments, and I return to their stories in chapter 4. I do not treat their stories as evidence for my own arguments but rather as a narrative context for them. I enjoyed multiple interactions with these students: I have known Helen and Cesar since that 2008 semester, when they were both enrolled in the same writing class, and I have known Nathan since 2010; I spoke with all of them at various times in recorded interviews, informal one-on-one conversations, in class, and on the phone; I taught each of them for at least one semester, and in Cesar's case, two; I communicate regularly with Cesar and Helen on Facebook and have used email to get in touch with all of them; I can still talk with Nathan in the halls outside my office. All of my history with these students informs my work here, and perhaps most significant to this project are the tremendous respect I have developed for each of them as well as my deeply felt hope that they each achieve the success and happiness they imagine for themselves.

Much of my representation of their stories comes from recorded interviews, which were transcribed by a professional transcriptionist; I use italics when I quote directly from the transcription. I also quote directly from the texts Cesar wrote in my class (with his permission). In those interviews, we covered several years of their lives, all the way from their earliest memories of schooling, and in some cases their families' lives before that, up until the moment of the interview. The span of this coverage in part explains why I do not use these stories as evidence; no one's memory is reliable enough to use as evidence without verification of details from numerous other sources. But my other reason for seeing their stories as context rather than evidence is because what matters more than what *actually* happened is how these students *understand* what happened, how they tell themselves and others the stories of their lives. As Susan Jarratt, Katherine Mack, Alexandra Sartor, and Shevaun Watson argue in their article "Pedagogical Memory: Writing, Mapping, Translating," "Remembering is an act of participation, a placing of oneself in a story in a particular way" (Jarratt et. al 2009, 49). Including their stories in this book is my attempt to invite them to participate in the discourse of retention—a discourse ostensibly about students, but that nonetheless is remarkably silent about students' lived experiences. Retention scholarship relies heavily on data about students, and most often, quantitative data in the form of test scores, GPAs, household income, credit hours, student debt, and so on. Researchers and institutions retrieve this data from data warehouses built specifically for this purpose. The interviews I conducted, especially as they were situated within a long, multifaceted relationship between interviewer and interviewee, were not designed simply to retrieve more data. Rather, as Jarratt et al. argue, "The interview generates as much as retrieves knowledge," a phenomenon they refer to as "pedagogical memory" (49). Memories recounted in interviews like the ones I conducted are pedagogical in two ways: "They are memories of learning in school but also *memories that should teach writing teachers and administrators who elicit them*" (50; italics added). I do not believe it is an exaggeration to say I learned the essential elements of my arguments in this book from listening to my students' stories.

These stories are not meant to be representative, and not only because methodologically the sample size is far too small. In fact, the more stories I might gather, the further I would be from any useful theoretical construct that might inform pedagogy or policy. A key point one learns when listening to students' stories about why they enrolled in college, their experiences when there, why they leave, and what happens next, is that nothing they say is usefully generalizable. Except perhaps in terms of the broadest demographic principles such as socioeconomic factors, each student's decision to leave or persist is the accumulation of countless details, each unique to their own lives. None of these details, I assert, can be formulated as a data point that correlates with retention policy. For example, in the cases of Helen, Cesar, and Nathan, there was no single, defining moment upon which their decision to leave college turned that could then be correlated to a program, faculty or staff member, or event that could have prevented them from leaving. In fact, technically, none of them *left* college, they simply did not register the following semester. This isn't a decision so much as a course of action (or inaction) that is always reversible; Nathan reversed this course when he decided to transfer to another college two years after he left the first.

For me these stories are important and interesting because they are *not* representative, because they demonstrate, in all their fascinating nuance, that retention in higher education is not a solvable problem in the way we have framed the questions. We ask, why do students leave? and what can we do get them to stay? I argue—after listening to my students' stories—that we need to be asking, How can we redesign higher education generally, and our writing pedagogy and curricula specifically, so that we educate every single student in our classrooms, even those who might leave?

CHAPTER 1: A STORY OF RETENTION RESEARCH

In chapter 1, I tell the story of Helen, one of the students I came to know through my own classroom and research. Whereas chapters 2, 3, and 4 culminate in students' stories, in chapter 1, I intentionally frame the chapter as Helen's story, in part to correct for the absence of student voices in this body of work. But I also put Helen's story up against dominant strains of the research on retention. Retention is a relatively new field, and it is somewhat fragmented; many research projects focus on either individual factors contributing to attrition, or perhaps on a few interrelated factors, or on individual solutions. For example, a study might consider factors that affect international students, financial factors, and the role of parents in Latino students' experience, or it might look at a new advising model or a cohort program for first-year students that saw increased retention rates. If there is a foundational text in this field, it would be Vincent Tinto's *Leaving College*, which I look at more closely in chapter 3. Tinto argues that retention is achieved when a student is successfully integrated into an institution, and a lot of research since his book was published considers ways institutions might help students achieve integration. There is also the arm of the field that deals with methodology, how to define and measure the various factors. Individual elements of Helen's story seem to confirm some of the retention research: for example, there is a correlation between high-school GPA and whether or not a student leaves college after one or two semesters, and this correlation seems to be verified in Helen's case. However, Helen's story is more than an accumulation of individual elements or data points that can be plotted on a graph of retention rates, and her story, taken as a whole, tends to undermine any explanatory or predictive power of these individual elements.

Therefore, Helen's narrative raises the much larger question of what we are to *do* about those moments of correlation. I believe that when those individual moments are abstracted from the whole story, the conclusions are inherently incomplete. And yet, programs and policies are built upon this retention data. For example, admissions offices use retention research to determine the cutoff GPA for acceptance. One dominant strain of my project is my argument that faculty in general, and writing instructors in particular, must be cautious, critical even, of retention efforts in their own institutions. Nationally, retention rates have not changed significantly, even with the recent dramatic increase in retention research; there appears to be very little we can *do* to prevent students from leaving college. The complexity of Helen's story helps illustrate why retention efforts tend to be, by and large, ineffective. More important, though, what our institutions are doing in the name of retention, though well intentioned in most cases, might actually run counter to our own pedagogical and political goals. Retention research, as a dominant element of the larger retention discourse that circulates in our colleges and universities, motivates and justifies initiatives that perpetuate the current structure of power in higher education. I take up this critique in chapter 2.

But Helen's story also illustrates the significance of the second dominant strain of my project. For teachers like me, reading her narrative next to the research raises more questions than it answers, questions about what our responsibilities are to students like Helen, who may or may not graduate from the college or university where we meet them; questions about what and how we should teach in our writing courses when we know some students may leave; questions about the purpose of higher education and whom this institution should serve. In other words, the issue of retention holds tremendous heuristic value, clarifying and reframing some of the central themes in our field. Rather than move from the critique of chapter 2 to a summary dismissal of the entire topic of retention, I argue that we must confront the reality that many of our students will leave before graduating, some to transfer to other schools, some to return after several months or years, some never to earn a degree. These students who leave compel us to rethink what we're doing in our institutions and our classrooms, and in chapters 3 and 4, I consider more carefully these implications. The topic of retention should help us focus on educating the students who are here *right now* rather than trying to prevent them from leaving. In this light, Helen's story also serves the purpose of reminding us just how fascinating, complicated, resourceful, and intelligent our students can be, and how deserving they all are of our efforts, regardless of the trajectory of their educational endeavors.

CHAPTER 2: THE SEDUCTION AND BETRAYAL OF THE DISCOURSE OF RETENTION

If writing professionals have specific reasons to pay attention to retention discourse as it circulates in our institutions, we also have specific resources, skills, and habits of mind to draw on to do so. In chapter 2, I pursue a more rigorous critique of the discourse of retention, using the methodology of critical discourse analysis (CDA). This methodology situates discourse, in this case the discourse of retention, at the intersection of broader social contexts and instances of language use. I've always been drawn to this methodology and find it very productive in the projects I pursue for a couple of reasons. First, it aligns well with the concerns of a rhetorician who aims to study how language works, and it allows me to exercise my expertise in language studies because of the emphasis on the analysis of specific texts. But also, CDA is a deliberately politicized methodology. As Norman Fairclough and Ruth Wodak explain, "What is distinctive about CDA [as a methodology] is both that it intervenes on the side of dominated and oppressed groups and against dominating groups, and that it openly declares the emancipatory interests that motivate it" (Fairclough and Wodak 1997, 259).

One way of understanding this project is to see it as primarily concerned with identifying and intervening in the oppressive structures that prevent some students from achieving what they set out to achieve in higher education. I imagined at the beginning of my study that I would be able to identify structures that could account for the reasons my students were leaving, and my goal was to figure out how to intervene, to determine what we, as faculty, could do differently to help more people stay enrolled in college. As chapter 1 demonstrates, primarily through Helen's story, this goal is far from simple. I assumed retention scholarship would prove useful, but while it is ostensibly about preventing students from leaving college, the discourse of retention functions in much more complicated, and not altogether positive, ways in the institution of higher education today. CDA enables me to turn the critical lens onto the discourse of retention in order to identify how, ironically, rather than intervening in the oppressive structures that prevent some students from achieving their goals, the discourse itself participates in maintaining the very same structures.

I argue in chapter 2 that the discourse of retention—manifested as it is in the reports, addresses to faculty and staff, charts of retention data, emails, instructions to committees, job descriptions, and so on that circulate on college campuses— functions effectively as part of the ideological work necessary to sustain the economic system emerging in late-capitalist higher education. The discourse of retention is not an isolated phenomenon but instead an element of the broader social context of the corporatization of higher education. I look at specific features of that corporatization —the reliance on contingent labor, the adoption of certain management practices, especially those influenced by the Total Quality Management movement, and the infiltration of promotional culture into higher education—to demonstrate how the discourse of retention is implicated here. Once I establish the contours of the broader social context of the discourse of retention in this chapter, I ground my analysis in specific texts: I examine two self-studies produced by my college as part of the accreditation process through the Higher Learning Commission of the North Central Association of Colleges and Schools, written ten years apart, and analyze discursive change across the intervening decade.

Retention is an effective element of the ideological work of the corporatization of higher education because it is extremely difficult for anyone—teachers, students, the public—to argue against the professed goal of helping students succeed in higher education. This difficulty is one reason I find retention to be worth studying, despite the ineffectiveness of most retention efforts and their insidious role in perpetuating the dominant and oppressive structures of higher education today. Retention is also and always about individual students, about why some leave and some stick around, even though these voices are too often suppressed in this discourse. At the end of chapter 2, therefore, I put my critique of the discourse of retention up against the story of Cesar. I cannot in any way endorse the way the discourse of retention functions to justify and motivate the more hurtful practices of the corporatization of higher education; however, to the extent that this discourse can also call our attention to students like Cesar, it is worth taking seriously. I believe stories like Cesar's, and the questions these stories raise, can ultimately help us use the discourse of retention to achieve the "emancipatory interests" that motivate this project.

CHAPTER 3: THE POSSIBILITY OF FAILURE

Chapter 3 takes up two interrelated issues: the first is the problem of the financial costs and benefits of a college education; the second is the way failure is individualized in the context of retention. The relationship between these two issues derives from the history of the idea of failure in our culture. At one point, only a business venture could fail—failure was a concept that, at least in popular discourse, did not apply to individuals or other areas of experience. However, in the nineteenth century, the concept shifted, and the ideology of failure that still dominates today arose: expressed concisely by Ralph Waldo Emerson, the assumption that underlies failure today is that "nobody fails who ought not to fail. There is always a reason, in the man, for his good or bad fortune" (qtd. in Sandage 2005, 46). Given the considerable cost of a college education, funded for most students through loans and other kinds of debt, enrolling in college is increasingly taken as a risk. A college degree typically realizes long-term benefits, both financial and otherwise, for those who earn one compared to those who have a high-school degree or less. However, for students who leave, the debt becomes a long-term liability, and the credits they earn do not realize enough financial benefits to offset the risk they took; even those students who transfer or return to college later lose credits and time to degree. For these students, leaving college is a kind of failed business venture. The amount of money some students spend is almost tragic, especially for those who leave before earning a degree, and too often we as faculty don't talk about this aspect of students' education; given the ideology of failure dominant today, it is too easy to brush off this kind of financial failure as an individual's moral failing. Moreover, this ideology of failure, which locates failure "in the man," might limit how we understand the problem of students leaving. In the context of retention, the ideology that "nobody fails who ought not to fail" is further perpetuated by the dominant paradigm in retention research: the work of Vincent Tinto. I study his seminal work, *Leaving College*, with a particular interest in understanding how we have come to understand attrition to be an *individual's* problem. We see this in retention efforts framed in terms of intervention or prevention. Tinto's model for retention, which has been duplicated, revised, and expanded throughout the country, is based on the assumption that a student leaves when that individual fails to integrate academically and socially into the college or university. The problem with Tinto's model and its descendants, and the programs and policies that arise from them, is that they only attempt to align the individual student more thoroughly with preexisting intellectual and social values of the institution. Nothing is done to change the nature of the institution itself, and this, I argue, is where the discourse of retention fails most thoroughly.

I recognize here a tension between the obligation for individuals to integrate themselves into the status quo of existing institutions and the possibility that these same individuals might provide the opportunity for institutions to fundamentally change, to become radically more inclusive. We see this same tension in the fields of basic writing and disability studies, and I draw on those fields to illustrate my point here. What the problems of retention can do for us is to clarify the current limits of higher education, how this institution is fundamentally exclusive. If we can move from seeing retention as an individual's problem to understanding it as an institutional problem, the problem of retention compels us to ask ourselves and others a difficult question: How committed are we to the proposal that everyone who enrolls should earn a degree? A real commitment entails radical changes.

The story of Nathan provides important nuances to the arguments I make in this chapter. He was not able to enroll in college right after high school, got a rewarding union job, was laid off during the economic collapse of 2008, spent a disastrous semester at a city college, and eventually enrolled at my institution. Money is always tight, and he admits that if the union job were available again, he might choose that route, but right now he hopes a college degree will provide him some measure of financial security. At the same time, when asked about the value or worth of a college degree, he steers the conversation away from money and talks about the people he has met, the way he has "expanded" his knowledge. Retention should not be about trying to prevent Nathan from leaving, or about trying to fit Nathan and his varied and changing goals, experiences, and talents into the existing structure of higher education. Retention should be about identifying the ways we need to change the institution and our individual pedagogies so that when Nathan is enrolled at various points in his life, he can continue to expand his knowledge without going broke.

CHAPTER 4: BEYOND RETENTION

In chapter 4, I begin to think about the implications of the issue of retention for writing pedagogy. One of the points I make in chapter 1 is that while there may be very little we can do to prevent our students from leaving, we have a lot more control over what we do when they're sitting in front of us in our classrooms. In this chapter, I develop this point further to explore how retention can compel us to revise our goals for first-year writing. I look at the question of *transfer* as it has been studied in our field, the question of what it is students take with them from our classrooms and apply to other situations. Not much, it turns out; at least this is the most common answer provided by the research on transfer in composition studies. However, much of the research has been limited to what students take with them into future college classes, and more specifically, what they take with them into future college classes in consecutive semesters at the same institution. Our research, in other words, has been dominated by chronos, by a concern about one intellectual skill leading predictably to the next. The issue of retention reminds us that the experience of higher education is much more porous for students than this methodological framework recognizes; this research on transfer does not account for students who leave, whether they transfer to other institutions, stop out for a while and return later, or never return.

When we do take these students into account, we must ask very different questions. I argue that it would be logistically, methodologically, even conceptually impossible to conduct any meaningful research about what students take from our writing classes into the varied contexts of their lives, whether they are headed to more college classes, to work in any number of industries, to work caring for family, to other educational institutions, or to lives as engaged citizens; in many cases, students are headed to all of the above. Research on transfer always assumes there is a target situation for which we are preparing students; in fact, much of the field of composition studies—our pedagogies, our curricula, our theories about language development, and our methodologies—is based on the assumption that we are preparing students for something else. Differences among our approaches in the field can be explained by the different target situations we imagine ourselves to be preparing students for. What the issue of retention reminds us is that there is no such identifiable target; there are multiple targets, and they're all moving.

Moreover, if target implies a future context, then the assumption that we are preparing students for something else is an even less adequate conceptual framework because many of our students, even while they are in our classrooms, occupy a number of other roles and spaces that involve writing to varying degrees.

Recognizing how transient our students are, how unpredictable their paths through higher education, compels us to reframe our goals in terms of kairos. We need to recognize the opportunities for our students that exist right now, in our classrooms. In chapter 4, then, I begin to lay out the terms of a kairotic pedagogy, an approach that takes advantage of who is in front of us right now, and I provide several examples of courses that might be motivated by kairos. Finally, I discuss our obligation as faculty to participate in designing an institution that educates *all* of our students, those who may not graduate from our institution in four years right alongside those who will.

I conclude this chapter, and the book, by returning to the stories of Helen, Cesar, and Nathan. One point of returning to their stories is to continue my project of infusing the discourse of retention with student voices; two of these students have since left my institution as of this writing, and as much as the discourse of retention is about students who leave college, there is very little information about what happens when they do. Where do they go? What do they do? And what do they write? Again, these stories are not meant to be evidence for any kind of definitive answers to these questions, nor are they meant to be representative of all students. Rather, they are meant to add texture to the arguments I make throughout the book. The other point of returning to their stories at the end is, paradoxically, to resist closure. The issue of retention tends to have a fairly firm perimeter, bounded by when a student enrolls in college on the one end and by when a student graduates or leaves on the other. The stories of Helen, Cesar, and Nathan do not have such clear boundaries; they are unfinished, perpetually rewritten. If the discourse of retention is to serve any purpose for us it will be to help us imagine how our institutions and classrooms might change and expand to account for our students' ongoing stories.

NOTES

1.   All student names are pseudonyms.
2.   Nathan was not a participant in the Student Faculty Partnership for Success Program; he was a student in a course I taught in fall 2010.

1

A STORY OF RETENTION RESEARCH

Helen is one of the toughest students I've ever taught. By this I mean that, at times, her demeanor is tough. Her language is tough. And she would admit parts of her background are pretty tough, too. I also mean she is probably one of the brightest, most earnest, most hardworking students I have ever met, and it was tough to teach her when I knew she was struggling with money and family and relationships and her vision for the future and her own sense of herself. She approached the writing and the reading with an enthusiasm that made our classroom time together a joy, but I also spent many hours outside the classroom dealing with her extracurricular challenges, exhausting the resources and services at my college, and trying to come to terms with my limits as an educator.

Put simply, research on student retention tries to determine why a student like Helen might leave college after one semester, why others stay, and whether or not there is anything we can do to influence these decisions; the goal of such research is to figure out ways to keep as many students as possible enrolled in a particular institution. But the issue of retention is hardly simple, and it raises some particularly compelling questions about our own roles as educators. Helen was a tough student to teach because I didn't face a day during the semester she was enrolled in my class without confronting these questions: Is higher education a right or a privilege? What is the purpose of higher education? What does "success" in college mean? And what role does writing instruction play in answers to these questions?

This chapter tells Helen's story. I got to know Helen both as a participant in the Student Faculty Partnership for Success program (which I describe in the introduction) and as a student in my Writing and Rhetoric course. Like the other students I discuss in this book, she also sat down for a long recorded and

DOI: 10.7330/9780874219319.c001

transcribed interview while she was still enrolled in my college. (I return to Helen's story in chapter 4, and in that chapter, I draw on a second interview, conducted two and a half years later.)[1]

On one hand, the peculiarities of Helen's experiences, behaviors, and personality traits undermine much of what we think we know about retention—who leaves and how to prevent that from happening—and thus her story lays the groundwork for a critique of the discourse of retention, which I continue in chapter 2. On the other hand, the picture that emerges of a bright and engaged student who drops out of college after one semester compels me to ask important questions about my goals as a writing instructor and my responsibilities to teach students like Helen who may never graduate, at least not from the college where I taught them, questions I take up in chapters 3 and 4.

Helen in many ways represents the larger population of students who are at risk for leaving college before graduation, who may or may not transfer to other institutions or return later to achieve the degree. We hear in her story many of the "risk factors" the data tell us to look for when trying to determine who might leave. She is representative, too, because, paradoxically, her story is unique—I believe it is nearly impossible to extrapolate from this one case any useful generalizations about retention. I am inclined to argue that all students are unique in this way. Getting to know her, like getting to know the other students I write about in this book, has taught me just how much we don't know, and how much we may never be able to know, about the reasons some students leave and other students stay.[2]

In this chapter, I put Helen's story next to a discussion of some of the dominant strains of retention scholarship. I begin with a brief history of retention research to provide some necessary context. Then, I juxtapose Helen's narrative with highlights from recent retention research in order to illustrate the difficulties of going back and forth between students' voices and research, the struggle to reconcile both of these discourses into one tidy narrative, and the disjointedness of our understanding of retention.

A BRIEF HISTORY OF RETENTION RESEARCH

The issue of retention occupies a growing body of research: Vincent Tinto asserts that "student retention is one of the most widely studied areas in higher education" (Tinto 2006–2007, 1). While the motivations for studying and trying to improve retention are varied, the assumption in this body of scholarship, and even among other academics who do not study retention, is almost always that retention is good. Some retention scholars focus on the benefits to individual students who remain in school until they achieve a college degree: "A bachelor's degree is no longer considered a potential stepping stone to a better life. It is the gatekeeper to myriad social and individual benefits, ranging from income, employment stability, and occupational prestige to engagement in civic and political activities" (Cabrera, Burkum, and LaNasa 2005, 155). Other retention scholars stress the benefits to society, both politically and economically, of educating as many people as possible: "An educated citizenry will keep the United States strong and vibrant. This, in essence, is what makes us a great nation and an example for others to follow" (Seidman 2005b, 315).

Still others focus on the benefits to the institutions themselves. It is perhaps this motivation, more than the others, that fuels administrations' support for retention scholarship and programs. Tinto explains this rationale in very clear terms:

> Today it is more important than ever for institutions to respond to the challenge of increasing student success. Forced to cope with tight, if not shrinking, budgets, institutions face mounting pressure to improve their rates of student retention and graduation. In many cases, this pressure reflects the movement of states to include graduation rates in a system of institutional accountability. In other cases, this pressure reflects the impact of widely publicized ranking systems that include graduation rates as one measure of "quality." In still other cases, this pressure mirrors the reality that increased student retention is critical to the stability of institutional budgets. (Tinto 2005b, ix–x; cf. Hossler 2006)

It is difficult to distinguish the various motivations for studying retention inasmuch as focusing on the benefits to individuals and society speaks to the whole purpose of higher education, and focusing on the financial implications of the retention problem speaks to institutions' ability to fulfill that purpose. Nevertheless, the extent to which retention efforts are funded by individual colleges and universities and supported by upper-level administrators is often dependent on the extent to which such efforts will realize financial gains in the form of tuition dollars, state funding, or future graduates' support as alumni.

According to Joseph B. Berger and Susan C. Lyon, retention, as an area of concern in higher education, did not exist in any significant way until the beginning of the twentieth century, and only in the last three or four decades has an identifiable body of scholarship emerged (Berger and Lyon 2005, 9). The tremendous expansion of higher education in the 1950s due in part to the GI Bill, as well as increased access to higher education made possible through other movements like civil rights and feminism, diversified the student population in ways most institutions were not prepared for. As Berger and Lyon explain,

> Attempts to promote access and diversity on college campuses led to many challenges, some of which were directly associated with the retention of students. Many campuses were unprepared to deal with a more diverse student body, and many were unable or unwilling to create supportive environments for students of color. Additionally, many students from underrepresented minority groups that were now allowed greater access to higher education had not been provided adequate educational preparation, given the inequities in school systems throughout America. As a result, retention rates were quite low for minority students. (Berger and Lyon 2005, 16)

Thus, much like the history of the field of composition studies, especially the development of process approaches and the subfield of basic writing, research on retention in the 1970s arose, in part, as a response to the struggles of institutions to respond to the needs of these new students. There was also a fear among college administrators that enrollment numbers would begin to flatten in the late 70s, and in anticipation of this decline, seminal work on retention by William Spady and Vincent Tinto was published then (Berger and Lyon 2005, 16–19).

In the 1980s, the trend in retention research and practice moved toward "enrollment management," informed by the Total Quality Management movement of the same era: admissions, student services, recruitment, financial aid, and institutional research were consolidated around the effort to bring students in and keep them there (Berger and Lyon 2005, 21). Efforts like these initiated the student-as-consumer model that dominates higher education today, a phenomenon I return to in chapter 2. The current financial climate in higher education is prompting even more interest in the reasons students leave. Since the 1990s, retention has emerged as one of the most researched areas in higher education today (6). Dissertations about retention in higher education have increased 35 percent from the period of 1988–1998 to the period of 1999–2009.[3] Likewise, the quarterly, peer-reviewed *Journal of College Student Retention: Research, Theory & Practice* began publication in 1999. What's more, this is an area of scholarship that has yielded retention "experts," consultants who promise to provide programs and initiatives that will improve an institution's retention rate. One study found that a sample of forty American colleges spent, on average, close to $10,000 on conferences, webcasts, research reports, and other information sources and a mean of approximately $25,000 on consulting services to improve student retention in one year (Survey of Student Retention Policies in Higher Education 2008, 18–19). These figures do not include all the money put into the actual programs or positions created specifically to address retention. In other words, retention is a growth industry. Tinto admits that "it would not be an understatement to say that student retention has become big business for researchers, educators, and entrepreneurs alike" (Tinto 2006–2007, 2). And like any good industry, the entrepreneurs create the need for their services. There have always been students who drop out, or transfer to other schools, and there have been economic crises before, too. What's different now is that there is a battalion of consultants and a plethora of products and services ready to address what we now see as a problem, and a buzzword, a body of scholarship, and conversations in popular media and on local campuses—a complex, multilayered discourse—to keep the problem front and center.

And this is part of my point here: in large part due to the emergence of the field of retention scholarship, we see a student like Helen as a problem to be solved. Her story reminds us that positioning students within the framework of "problem: solution" is inadequate, unproductive, and possibly unethical.

RETENTION AND PREVIOUS ACADEMIC EXPERIENCES:
I WAS REALLY SCREWING MYSELF HARD AS HELL.

Helen's story is punctuated by her many moves. During high school, she lived in the city, then moved out to a suburb with her mom, where, in her words, *I got Saturday detentions almost every weekend. Didn't go . . . I wasn't going to classes. I was ditching a lot of the morning classes, always late.* She got involved with gangs, then moved out to her dad's home to avoid the gang members after her close friend (and gang brother) was killed and they were coming after her. About that school, she said, *They threw me into geometry. And geometry I slept through every day. I told the* [teacher] *I'm not going to be able to learn this. And I slept through it every day. Chemistry was the same thing, slept through that. So, like, I was really screwing myself hard as hell, hard as hell. I wasn't passing any classes.*

She then moved back to her mom's because she found out she wouldn't graduate on time from the school she attended at her dad's. When asked if she had been held back a year in school because of all the turbulence, she replied, *In answer to your question if I was held back, technical I was held back because when I went to H-F as a junior, they did label me as a sophomore, so I guess that is being held back. But they told me I'd be able to make up the credits. But they're telling me in order to graduate, I would have to do so much schoolwork, Prairie State College to do night courses, do this, and then get my diploma mailed to me. I told them, kiss my ass. Either I'm going to graduate on time, or instead of doing all this stuff, I'll get my GED because it will be a lot quicker than doing all the extra shit.* Rather than go to that trouble, she reenrolled in her original high school and, in her words, *I killed my senior year. Killed it. Came out with As and Bs. Killed it. Graduated on time.*

According to Jennifer L. Crissman Ishler and M. Lee Upcraft's review of retention literature, "There is substantial evidence that the most powerful predictor of persistence into the sophomore year is the first-year student's prior academic achievement, including high school grades" (Ishler and Upcraft 2005, 33; see also Astin and Oseguera 2005, 256; Caison 2004–2005, 431). If "prior academic achievement" can predict whether or not a student will reenroll after the first semester or first year of college, then Helen's high-school experience does not bode well. Her high-school GPA undoubtedly reflected all of the moving around and violence and uncertainty that characterized her life during this period of time. Regardless of the quality of her high schools or the availability of AP classes or extracurriculars, she clearly wasn't taking advantage of opportunities to prepare for college academically or behaviorally, and that lack of preparation is to some degree captured in the GPA numbers.

However, what her GPA doesn't adequately reflect is her high intelligence or her tough personality, which one can see glimpses of in her narrative here, and which I witnessed in the classroom and in interactions with Helen over the course of several years. Many writing program administrators are understandably wary of GPAs and SATs and all of their numbers as indicators of intelligence or writing ability. To this general sense of wariness I'll add the further caution that when these numbers are used to predict retention, they'll increasingly be used to determine access (an institution determined to improve retention numbers will be more likely to deny access to students whose numbers suggest they won't make it) (see my discussion of Astin in chapter 2).

What is unnerving for me, in trying to understand retention better, is how even knowing more of Helen's story, even seeing behind the numbers, even coming to tremendously enjoy and respect her intelligence and her personality, I am no better able to predict her chances of graduating from college.

RETENTION AND THE ROLE OF THE FAMILY:
I TOLD YOU THIS WASN'T GOING TO WORK.

With the encouragement of a friend, Helen applied to Columbia College Chicago, a private generous-admissions arts and media college. Her acceptance was contingent on attending a Summer Bridge program: *Yeah, and I got a letter that said I had to do the Bridge program, and I was pissed. I remember I was pissed about that. My mom read the letter first, though, and out of her mouth was, I told you this wasn't going to work and all this. But I was pissed, like, man, I wrote good on that essay. There should be no reason. But then I thought about it. They probably looked at my high school and, you know, my test scores, and they probably figured, you know. But I couldn't blame them for that because I wasn't showing up, so what the—you know? So, I told my mom—she told me I couldn't do it, and I said, watch.*

When asked if she had either of her parents' support when she started the Bridge program, she answered immediately: *No. My dad, like, he did come with me one time to another open house, like, after I came with* [a friend] *and stuff. It was like a parent thing. He came with me, and he said he liked the school, and he liked it because the music—neither one of my parents supported it as a career for me, or, you know what I'm saying, where I should be going to school at. But they're still—to this day, they're still talking about me going to community college.*

Like her previous academic experiences and high-school GPA, Helen's parents might be considered a "risk factor." It seems like common sense, but retention scholars confirm that "students whose parents expressed belief in their competence and abilities and who shared the students' interests and concerns were more likely to perform well in college than those whose parents did not demonstrate these attributes" (Cutrona et al. 1994, 373). Not only did her parents not support her college choice, but her mother, from the very beginning, showed very little confidence in Helen's ability to succeed.

A college or university studies retention for one of two reasons: either to prevent students from leaving, or to predict who is likely to leave and prevent those students from enrolling in the first place. In either case, why study factors like students relationships with their parents? This is something institutions can neither predict nor control. Perhaps knowing Helen's story of her relationship with her parents helps, in some small way, to explain her performance, both in high school and college, but it actually raises more questions than it answers. For example, when and how do we intervene if we feel a student's mom is eroding her sense of confidence and accomplishment, and thus her chances to succeed? In the context of retention efforts, should an institution's approach to *in loco parentis* take into account students who have very little emotional or financial support from their parents? *In loco parentis* is the idea that the university should play the role of the parent while the student is on campus. This idea was challenged successfully in the 1960s and 1970s when students demanded more autonomy and more prominent roles in college governance, and when the legal age to vote was lowered to eighteen. At this point, colleges and universities shifted away from a culture of *in loco parentis.* However, more recently, institutions have been sued and found responsible for things that have happened to students while on campus. The tendency of parents to sue institutions, as well as the culture of "helicopter parenting," has initiated another shift, back toward policies and practices that might be understood as *in loco parentis.* Some retention efforts—including our own Student Faculty Partnership for Success program—could be seen as efforts by the institution to play the role of the parent; I believe we need more research and greater skepticism when this occurs (see Trimbur (2000), as well as Podis and Podis (2007), for critiques of *in loco parentis* in composition studies.)

Students' relationships with their parents provide some of the most dissonant moments in the juxtaposition of retention scholarship and individual students' stories. Helen's relationship with her mother, or, at times, the lack thereof, was, in my mind, perhaps the single most disruptive force in Helen's academic career. And yet, no amount of research about this topic, no type of retention program, can do anything to change this situation.

RETENTION, SELF-EFFICACY, AND INSTITUTIONAL SUPPORT: *I REALLY DIDN'T HAVE ANY SAY-SO.*

Even though her mother discouraged her, Helen did enroll in the Bridge program, where she met Danielle. Helen was very successful in the program and agreed to partner with Danielle in the Student Faculty Partnership for Success program. We asked Helen whether she felt ready for the semester after completing the Bridge program. *Yeah, I was, but then no. I don't know. I was, but then I was nervous because I'm thinking, okay, if that was two classes with Bridge, now I'm taking five. And that ended up being my worst—you know what I'm saying, like, that ended up being what kicked me in the ass in the end.*

Helen enrolled in fifteen credit hours for her first semester at Columbia. *I didn't even choose any of my classes. This lady, I don't even know her name, but this lady just sat me at a computer and she did everything. She told me what* [classes] *to pick out and what to pull. So, I really didn't have any say-so in what classes I wanted to take, really.* It was in the Art of Business Recording, a class required for Helen's major, that she started questioning whether or not she wanted to continue her degree in Music Business. *Because we had, like, a paper, a sixteen-page paper due on—what was it like, the different—I showed you, the different jobs. And I have to talk about how country and rap did this in the industry and how money and all, like—it just wasn't—when I looked at that paper, I was like, well, this is my career. I should love doing this. And I showed, you know, David in our class, I showed him the paper, and he was like, man, maybe I should do this. I would love to write a paper like that. So, I'm thinking, like, damn, you know, people actually like doing this, so maybe this ain't for me. And that was just—and another reason why I dropped* [the class] *was because that was just—I already saw a downfall. You know. I already saw that it was going to bring me down, so I just figured, just cut it while I can, you know?*

While faculty may be the most obvious point of contact between a student and the institution, Helen's story also highlights how multifaceted the student's college experience is. She was nervous going in—retention scholars would identify this as her lack of a sense of self-efficacy (Bean 2005, 220–23). And while it might be tempting to ascribe this nervousness to her prior academic experiences or to her relationship with her parents, one might also consider how the institution could have exacerbated her nervousness. As John P. Bean says, "Any interaction between students and an institution's faculty and other employees that increases the students' sense of self-efficacy is likely to improve their attitudes toward school and increase their likelihood of remaining enrolled" (221). The fact that Helen didn't get much say in shaping her first-semester schedule undoubtedly failed to increase her sense of self-efficacy. Moreover, as she became increasingly unsure about her career choice and major, she could surely have benefitted from better academic advising. Tinto argues that "advising is particularly important to the success of the many students who either begin college undecided about their major or change their major during college" (Tinto 2005a, 322).

I understand the importance of institutional efforts to improve students' experiences with academic advising, the financial aid office, and other crucial services. And I think Helen's experience with these services at my college should have been better. However, I am not confident that improved services would necessarily increase her chances of succeeding. The more I know of her story, the less able I am to identify straightforward solutions: Improve the advising process! Provide more career counseling! Tutoring! Better customer service in Financial Aid! I see how a student's sense of self-efficacy and her chances for success are the accumulation of variables both as profound as the relationship between mother and daughter, for example, and as capricious as an academic advisor's bad day, a chance conversation with a classmate, the timing of the withdraw date on the academic calendar.

RETENTION AND THE ROLE OF FACULTY:
I JUST FELT LIKE SHE REALLY DIDN'T CARE.

Helen was also realizing that, unlike during the Bridge Program, which provided intensive interactions with instructors, she had to initiate relationships with her teachers. She admitted she didn't always make the effort to do this. She admitted that she never went to the office of two of her instructors but communicated primarily through email: *Just through email and my—but with my econ teacher, I'll leave him a—like, I haven't—me and him haven't been—he only knows, like, a fragment of what's been going on in my life, you know? And I'm sure when he reads an email, and I tell him I've got a lot going on, it doesn't faze him, you know? But he—I told him about the car accident. I told him about that. But I really haven't—I didn't go in detail like I should have, you know? But I didn't feel that—to me, he wasn't that kind of teacher to give you that connection to chitchat like that, you know?*

And of the other teacher, Helen explained, *She knows everything, but it's like she rushed, like, when I was trying to explain to her, because I came up—I sent her an email when I was absent for the classes. And one day after class, I went up to her and I wanted to talk to her personally and just explain to her personally, like, everything I said in the email, but to her face. And when I was talking to her and she was, like, oh, like rushing me, like, oh, it's okay! Yeah, it's okay . . . you know? So, I just felt like she really didn't care. She seemed—she told me I'm going to pass, so that's what it was, you know?*

A student's relationship with faculty can have profound consequences and yet be the result of the capriciousness of the registration process. In their review of retention scholarship, Ishler and Upcraft refer to a study that found that "specific faculty behaviors contributed to student persistence: faculty members being supportive of student needs, being approachable, and returning telephone calls and e-mails in a timely fashion" (Ishler and Upcraft 2005, 38; cf. Lundquist, Spalding, and Landrum 2002/2003). Increasingly, retention scholars—and my college administration—are arguing for the role of faculty in improving students' chances of success. Tinto and other leading retention scholars are increasingly convinced that "the actions of the faculty, especially in the classroom, are key to institutional efforts to enhance student retention" (Tinto 2006–2007, 5). In one (unintentionally) humorous article about retention, the authors study the correlation between humor and student success, and one of their recommendations is that "universities and colleges could hold seminars, colloquiums, and other methods of teaching and training faculty members the importance of incorporating humor into the classroom setting" (Hickman and Crossland 2004–2005, 241). Faculty might do well to join the conversation about retention before some well-meaning administrator requires attendance at clown college as part of faculty development.

What first-year writing faculty do as a matter of course—teach smaller classes, conduct frequent conferences, assign papers that call for personal writing—is a tremendous resource, deliberately or not, for retention efforts at their institutions. But, in spite of—or is it because of?—my experience getting to know students like Helen and the others I discuss in this book, I am hesitant to argue that this is a role that faculty should seek or fill. What should be the extent of faculty response-ability? Just how "supportive" and "approachable" should we be? These are sincere questions, arising out of a real frustration with the conflict between my best intentions and my most severe limitations. Because of my role in the Student Faculty Partnership for Success program, I found myself, over the course of the single semester I was teaching Helen and her cohort, trying to respond to domestic violence, the threat of homelessness, financial crises, possible unplanned pregnancies, mental illnesses, physical illnesses, and a whole host of other serious issues confronted by the students in the program. I was overwhelmed and underqualified. Even when I am not actively participating in retention research as I was that semester, I regularly face dilemmas about whether and how to intervene in situations that are negatively affecting my students' work in my class. Events at Virginia Tech, and closer to home, Northern Illinois, have raised a whole host of legal and ethical issues about faculty response-ability. In the context of those tragedies, retention seems almost trivial.

It is easy to point an accusatory finger at the faculty member who was too rushed to talk with Helen, or who didn't like to "chitchat." But I am that faculty member sometimes, too. Moreover, I could never argue that faculty should play a more prominent role in responding to student needs in the name of retention until the working conditions of our part-time colleagues are drastically improved. It should be obvious to all readers that teachers' working conditions and students' experiences at any given institution are inextricably linked. However, Tony Scott argues that "discussions of academic labor and writing program management rarely touch on the specific effects of faculty hierarchies and pervasive managerialism on day-to-day pedagogy" (Scott 2005, 38). Should the discussions Scott calls for here ever take place, it is important that we consider retention efforts, too. It is the part-time faculty, after all, who so often end up shouldering much of this responsibility. In the case of my institution, I found that—due to both staffing scenarios and the enthusiastic involvement of newer teachers—many of the part-time faculty members developed lasting bonds with our students and tried, endlessly and without additional compensation, to facilitate success during these students' first year. (See chapter 2 for a longer discussion of the relationship between contingent labor and the discourse of retention.)

RETENTION AND STRESS, TIME, AND MONEY:
IT TAKES [A] TOLL ON YOUR MIND AFTER A WHILE.

Helen's first-semester experience, and her frustrations, were heavily influenced by events happening outside the classroom, including the fact that her need for money, both to pay for school and to live, required that she work twenty to thirty hours a week as a janitor at a suburban mall. When asked what were the top three factors that contributed to her not doing as well as she wanted in her classes, her first response came quickly: *Time. Time is one. That's one thing I can say. Like, I didn't give enough time in my studies . . . I did not give enough time in my studies. But that's because I didn't have the time.*

She continued, naming the second factor: *Well, just drama, like, just drama at my house, and just like the situation. I mean, my family and, like, as stupid as it sounds, but with me jumping a lot with different houses, it really, it takes toll on your mind after a while, like, not having, like, one bed to sleep in. Like, it sounds really stupid. I mean, that sounds lame as hell, but—well, like, I don't know. To me, it just sounds like a bad reason not to, like, do good in school, but just jumping around and having to worry about, like, one month having the money for a Metra pass but then next month not having the money for a Metra pass, but then where am I going to stay, and not argue, you know? It was just—that's one thing I feel.*

She needed to be prompted to list the third factor; "Is it money, then?" we asked. Helen hesitated: *Yeah. That would be it. Well, I wouldn't even say the money, like, would affect the grades, because money comes and goes, you know? . . . I would say number three stress, then. Yeah.*

So, how does a faculty member, who is worried about time, money, family obligations, and the stress of day-to-day living, respond to these concerns in a student? Worries about time and money converge for most students in an unavoidable Catch-22: the absolute necessity of a job to pay for school, and the time a job takes away from schoolwork. It is interesting to note that Helen doesn't really consider money to be a top stressor. *Money comes and goes, you know?* But neither does she consider it an option to *not* work, and the time commitment required of working is, in her mind, the number-one stressor. Part-time work (fewer than fifteen hours) on campus has been found to increase a student's chances of persisting. More hours, or work off campus, decreases these chances (Ishler and Upcraft 2005, 39). But on-campus work is not available for everyone, and most students, like Helen, need far more hours to barely scratch by. It's tempting to see money as the cure-all for all attrition. However, even this solution isn't as simple as it looks. While more money probably would make a huge difference for Helen, I heard too many stories from other students for whom money was not the reason they were struggling. Moreover, retention scholars argue that it's not just a student's ability to pay for school that influences retention, but if students believe the cost *exceeds the benefits*, they may decide to leave (Braxton and Hirschy 2005, 62).

The stressors Helen names are fairly typical. At times, the stress she was under might have been different in degree, but not necessarily different in kind, than the stress all of our students and our colleagues experience. So why does this stress prevent some people from succeeding while others are able to manage? And to what extent can retention efforts deal with these factors?

RETENTION AND PLAIN BAD LUCK:
I HAD NO REASON TO SCREAM.

So I wasn't, like, steady living at Mom's house, but I was there most of the time now. And the first two weeks, we were just bickering. The third week, it was horrible. And then around that time, I got in the car accident. It was on a Wednesday night, and—I got in the car accident, and my parents, like, I don't know. They weren't focused on the car accident. They were focused on the neighborhood I was in. Which it wasn't—it was on Seventy-Sixth and State, and my house is on Eighty-Seventh. So, really, you know what I'm saying, you can't really bitch at me for that. You know? . . . Well, I go home, and my mom—I already called my parents when the accident happened. And I go home and I talk to my mom. I said I need—because she was holding $400 for me. She had $400 of my savings. And so I said I need $100 to get the car—to tow the car. When I got to the curb, she was gone. She went with her boyfriend and left the money on the table. Which right there, that kind of hurt my feelings because if it was me and my daughter got into an accident, my ass would be waiting outside for her to come through that door. You know what I'm saying?

And then the next day, well, I got home to the house. After all this, got home to the house, and my mom goes, where's your laptop? that I just got that Tuesday before. This is Wednesday. I got it the week before on Tuesday. And I said, what? And she said, where's your laptop? And I said, you're taking away my laptop? And she goes, not me, your father.

The next day, I wake up to both my parents calling off of work. And I go outside, and my dad's there, and he sees my car, and I could see his whole face turn pale. And he gets to where he about threw up. And I looked at him and said, at least I'm not dead. You know? That's all I could say. I didn't know what to say, you know? My car looked horrible. And he was just like, don't talk to me right now. And I said, okay, that's fine. I just walked away, and I came back about ten minutes later, and I said, well, what am I going to do about my car? And he looked at me, and his white face turned to red, and he started screaming at me, telling me how I'm fucking up my life, how he don't know what's going on in my head or what I'm doing. And I just—I, at that point, like, with the accident and everything, I had no energy. I had no reason to scream.

The story that Helen tells about the car accident illustrates perfectly the bewildering mess of issues that comprise the problem of retention: the family drama, again; unexpected expenses that eat into savings; missed days at work and school because of transportation; even access to technology (because of her work schedule and commute to school, she did not have enough time in the labs on campus to do homework; the laptop, a gift from her father, promised to be a real boost to her performance in school).

And all of this triggered, by chance, an unlucky wrong-place-wrong-time occurrence. The car accident, for Helen, was a turning point, the point at which I saw her motivation, her self-confidence, and her energy levels drop precipitously. Up until that point, the Student Faculty Partnership for Success program had provided her with a valuable support network, which, combined with her intelligence and wit and strong will, made all those who worked with Helen, and Helen herself, hopeful. But there is no retention research or well-intentioned faculty member or institutional program that could have prevented or predicted this accident. And if Helen does not enroll in subsequent semesters, then she is left with no college degree and serious amounts of debt. While her relationship with my college may dissipate, the consequences of the few months she was here could plague her for years.

There are a number of details in Helen's story that could be plotted as data points in a retention study: her high-school GPA, her family background, her experience in the advising office, her relationship with faculty, her income, and so on. But very little in her story tells us what we should do differently, as faculty or as institutions. This conclusion is consistent with the retention scholarship at large. Tinto acknowledges that "while it can be said that we now know the broad dimensions of the process of student leaving, we know very little about a theory of action for student persistence" (Tinto 2005a, 317). We might be able to explain the reasons some students leave and some succeed, and in some cases we might even be able to predict these outcomes with some degree of accuracy, but we still don't know what to do about it.

RETENTION AND WRITING INSTRUCTION:

I'M GOING TO GRADUATE EVENTUALLY. JUST EVENTUALLY.

Helen was asked, on a scale of 1 to 10, 10 being the most sure, how sure was she that she was going to graduate from our college in the next five years. She replied, 7 . . . *I would say 10, but the thing is, I'm just not sure if I want to keep to music. You know. But I have to do something from Columbia because I don't see myself being at any other college, so I have to pick some kind of degree to graduate, so 7 1/2, but we'll push it to 10, though, because I'm going to graduate eventually.* [CHUCKLES] *Just eventually. But I do know for a fact that if I don't have my stuff together by the age of, like, twenty—I said twenty-one, but I'm saying twenty—I'm going to the military. I already—I have no other option. And I figure twenty-one will be a good age, because by the time I serve four years, I'll still come out young, you know? I won't have any—I don't know. That's it.*

And yet, we must continue to teach, knowing that there are other Helens in our classrooms (we should be so lucky!), and that every student deserves our best efforts. The one factor in Helen's experiences I don't discuss in the sections above is her time in my classroom. This is the one factor that we writing instructors *do* control, that we *can* predict, at least to some extent, with thoughtful lesson plans and assignment design. I argue that the issue of retention should frame our thinking about pedagogy more than it currently does: What should our course goals be when we consider that many of our students may leave our institution after they take our class, some never to return, others to graduate from other institutions, others to return in a couple of years?

My response is that we need to stop thinking of our first-year courses, and especially basic-writing courses (which are more likely to be populated by students who are at risk for dropping out), as *preparation* for further academic study. In other words, we need to stop privileging chronology in our curriculum, the principle that *first* they learn this so that *then* they can learn that. It is counterintuitive, I realize, to dismiss this principle because many informed and well-intentioned first-year writing and basic-writing pedagogies are grounded in the assumption that if only we give students a solid foundation (of basic skills, of critical thinking, of academic strategies), they will succeed. However, in the context of retention, keeping in mind students like Helen who, for a whole host of other reasons, may never take another college course—or who may graduate *just eventually*—it is even more important that we design courses that are meaningful for what students do right now, while they're in our classrooms. Such courses are less chronological and more kairotic.

As I say early in this chapter, Helen's story is representative of all our students' stories because, paradoxically, it is unique. Carolyn R. Miller argues that "*kairos* is understood to represent not the expected but its opposite: the uniquely timely, the spontaneous, the radically particular" (C. Miller 2002, xiii). Helen's story is filled with, to revise Miller's phrase, radical particulars. To serve students like Helen, to do justice to their time in our classrooms, we must think of our pedagogy and curricula in terms of kairos. Miller continues, "This sense of kairos encourages us to be creative in responding to the unforeseen, to the lack of order in human life. The challenge is to invent, within a set of unfolding and unprecedented circumstances, an action (rhetorical or otherwise) that will be understood as uniquely meaningful within those circumstances" (xiii). Research on retention is designed to predict and control the radical particulars of the experiences of students like Helen. Immersed as I was in the discourse of retention, much of my approach to her various situations that semester, if not motivated by an attempt to predict and control, was at least motivated by an attempt to react or to fix. How much more productive if I had approached my pedagogy and my interactions with her as an opportunity to "be creative," as a "challenge to invent" both rhetorical and pedagogical actions that could have been "uniquely meaningful within those circumstances."

Helen did leave Columbia College, the college where she was a student in my first-year writing course. She left after her first semester. As of this writing she has no plans to reenroll at Columbia. I take up her story again in chapter 4, but my point here is not about the rest of her story. Rather, my point is that despite the risk factors in her background, there was no way to predict with 100 percent certainty that she would leave, and I strongly believe that neither was there any way to prevent her from leaving. What I can do for students like her is to focus my energies on educating them while they are in front of me. This is not a matter of limiting the purview of my responsibility for retention but rather recognizing the enormity of my responsibility *as a writing instructor* and taking advantage of the opportunities to invent meaningful pedagogical actions in response to the "lack of order in human life."

My immersion in the discourse of retention and my work with students who are most at risk for leaving before graduation have led me to revise my approach to teaching more than they have led me to revise any particular method I might enact. Rather than advocate for types of assignments or classroom activities, I want to advocate for seeing teaching through the lens of kairos: What is going on in my students' lives *right now* to which we might use writing as a meaningful response? What are the conversations and texts circulating in our college or our community *now* that my students could participate in through writing? What do I need to teach them about rhetoric and writing that would enable them to respond and participate more productively? And how might I build moments into my syllabus that we can open up to allow for the unpredictable forces in my students' lives? Seeing through this lens isn't so much a method as a deliberate stance, a commitment to be inventive, a willingness to see each semester as "a time that marks an opportunity which may not recur" (John E. Smith

2002, 47). I return to a fuller discussion of a kairotic pedagogy in chapter 4.

In composition studies, we've always understood our work to occupy an important liminal space situated between students' homes and the academy. The issue of retention multiplies the contexts with which our work intersects when we recognize that students may leave the academy soon after, sometimes even during, our course. Thus, this project is ultimately motivated not by my frustration with the research and my critique of the larger discourse of retention, but by the way Helen's story has completely revised the way I approach my work as a writing instructor.

NOTES

1. An earlier version of this chapter was coauthored by Danielle Aquiline, who taught Helen in our college's summer Bridge Program and stayed in touch with Helen throughout her semester at Columbia and beyond. Danielle also participated in the first interview. Danielle has read and agreed to my representation of our interactions with Helen, but she is not responsible for any possible oversights or poor judgment about word choice.

2. I first interviewed Helen with Danielle Aquiline on campus on December 11, 2008; that conversation was transcribed by a professional transcriptionist. All of Helen's words appear here, in italics, exactly as they appear in the transcript. An ellipsis (. . .) indicates parts of the conversation that were not included; brackets with italics inside [*italics*] indicate places where I inserted words to protect someone's anonymity, or because Helen's words weren't clear on the tape and I inserted a word that was our best guess. I used regular font to indicate my narrative explanations in Helen's story, as well as my review of the scholarship and my own reflections.

3. A search in the Dissertation Abstracts database, with the keyword *retention* and the subject heading *education, higher*, from 1988–1998, yielded 877 results. The same search in the years 1999–2009 yielded 1,190 results.

2

THE SEDUCTION AND BETRAYAL OF THE DISCOURSE OF RETENTION

I have begun to understand that students leaving my college before they graduate is less a problem I need to solve and more an occasion for me to be creative, an opportunity to invent meaningful pedagogical responses to the unique forces circulating in their lives and in my classroom. However, from an institutional perspective, the goal of retention research is still to prevent students from leaving, regardless of the possibility that such efforts may be futile: as the idiosyncrasies of Helen's story illustrate, each student's background and experiences create a unique complex of factors, so there are few—if any—institutional responses that can address the whole of an individual student's situation; much less likely is the chance that a single program, single staff or faculty member, or single institutional effort could address all students' unique situations and thus prevent large numbers of students from leaving.

In fact, no one knows how to prevent attrition. According to one review of the relevant data at the national level, "College graduation rates for those who start college may be decreasing or increasing, depending on the data set used. Or, if one uses the longest data set (from the Census Bureau), college graduation rates may be unchanged over the last fifty years" (Mortenson 2005, 43). In other words, even after seventy-five years of research, and a dramatic increase in the quantity of scholarship about retention in the last couple of decades, rates of attrition haven't increased nationally, but neither have rates of retention (Braxton, Brier, and Steele 2007–2008, 377; see also Seidman 2005b, 295).

I do not want to be totally defeatist. After all, *trying* to help students persist, even when that immediate goal fails, may

DOI: 10.7330/9780874219319.c002

still have positive implications for the institution and for students themselves. For example, it is difficult to argue against improved counseling services or more resources going toward tutoring initiatives, even if there is no measurable correlation with increased retention rates. But given the reluctance even among retention scholars to claim that all this talk about retention has helped—for example, Alan Seidman's incredulity is clear: "Logic dictates that the addition of programs and services should improve the retention of students, but in reality this seems not to be the case" (Seidman 2005a, xii)—how do we explain the endurance, and in fact, increased intensity, of this discourse? Such an explanation is impossible if we consider retention as an isolated phenomenon, if we fail to understand the relationship between the discourse of retention and the broader social context of higher education. In chapter 4 I return in earnest to the effects my research on retention has had on my teaching. While I am never too far from the classroom in this and the next chapter, my purpose here is to articulate the ways in which the broader discourse of retention intersects with the material and political contexts in which we do the work of writing program administration and composition instruction. I argue here that the discourse of retention is both a product of broader social changes surrounding higher education as well as a site of tension within, or evidence of ambivalence about, if not resistance to, these changes.

In this chapter, I illustrate the points I am making about the relationship between the broader social context of higher education and the discourse of retention with references to the way this conversation has played out on my campus. When I refer to the *discourse of retention,* I am using *discourse* deliberately here. My analytical approach is very much indebted to the work of Norman Fairclough in the 1990s and his colleagues in critical discourse analysis (CDA), so I will use the term *discourse* here for the sake of methodological precision. However, it would not be too much of a stretch to refer to the *rhetoric of retention* rather than the *discourse of retention.* In his 2000 book about the language of Britain's New Labour party, written for a broader readership than his theoretical and methodological texts, Fairclough himself makes the connections between rhetoric and discourse (Fairclough 2000, 16). Perhaps reflecting the popular usage of his intended audience, he begins by using *rhetoric* dismissively: in the first line of his preface, for example, he asks, "Is New Labour's 'new politics' for a 'new Britain' *just rhetoric, just empty words*" (vii; italics added) and he seems to be pitting rhetoric against "substance" (viii). However, in chapter 6, he uses the methodology of CDA to reverse this reductive understanding of rhetoric and to closely align the concerns of rhetorical analysis and CDA. He explains in that chapter that what is generally perceived as a dichotomy between reality and rhetoric is better understood as "some rather complex relationships" between a variety of elements of political action, including between "language as part of the action and other parts of the action" (145).[1]

Here, I find CDA useful to study the relationship between specific retention efforts—the actions undertaken by an institution to enroll a student until graduation—and how we *talk and write about* the complex of issues surrounding retention, student success and failure, efforts to retain students, and our reasons for doing so. Following Fairclough and the methodology of CDA, I study the discourse of retention in specific texts, namely written documents and conversations about retention that circulate in my own institution. In CDA, sentence-level details and the ideological implications of these details are theoretically and methodologically connected through the concept of discourse. Fairclough, a key figure in the field of CDA scholarship, situates himself between, on one hand, linguistic and sociolinguistic approaches to discourse analysis, and on the other hand, social, theoretical approaches such as that of Michel Foucault. In so doing, Fairclough argues for a view of discourse as "a mode of political and ideological practice":

> Discourse as a political practice establishes, sustains, and changes power relations, and the collective entities (classes, blocks, communities, groups) between which power relations obtain. Discourse as an ideological practice constitutes, naturalizes,

sustains and changes significations of the world from diverse positions in power relations. (Fairclough 1992, 67)

Fairclough asserts that discourse constitutes social structure in both conservative and innovative ways; that is, discourse is not merely the function of those in power as they reproduce their power but also is the function of those who challenge and change the nature of that power. While discourse constitutes social structure in multiple ways, Fairclough further emphasizes the dialectical relationship between discourse and society (Fairclough 1992, 65). Current elements of the social structure—gender, race, class, identities based on place, type of government, for example—shape profoundly the ways that discourses function.

What CDA adds to the Foucauldian view of discourse is the conviction that a focus on language is necessary to the study of discourse. Again, this is where I see the alignment between rhetoric and CDA. According to Fairclough, discourse is always manifested in actual language use, specific spoken or written texts: "If being an instance of social (political, ideological, etc.) practice is one dimension of a discursive event, being a text is another" (Fairclough 1992, 71). In this book, therefore, when I refer to the *discourse of retention*, I am signifying a configuration of textual and social practices. I am talking about the ways the language, arguments, rhetorical tropes, and genres surrounding retention function politically and ideologically. The discourse of retention works through conversations on campuses, marketing materials, statistical data and the analysis and representation of that data, scholarly articles, job descriptions that specify responsibility for retention, and so on. In all these examples, people take actions through the discourse of retention—they might justify hiring or firing faculty and staff, or market the college to potential students/consumers, or persuade an accrediting agency that the college is viable. To study the discourse of retention is to explicate how discourse might contribute to these effects. Still, the discourse of retention, as I use the word *discourse*, is always manifested in particular texts that the critical-discourse analyst can study—conversations, marketing materials, reports.

In this chapter, I first discuss the social context of the discourse of retention, focusing on the corporatization of higher education. Then I study how this larger context is evident in the details of two key institutional texts that circulated at my own college—the self-studies, written ten years apart, that were produced as part of the re-accreditation process. Finally, as I do in all the chapters of this book, I tell an individual student's story in order to ground my larger arguments in the specifics of real students' educational experiences.

UNDERSTANDING THE SOCIAL CONTEXT OF THE DISCOURSE OF RETENTION

The discourse of retention illustrates contradictory impulses present in contemporary higher education: although we like to think higher education is designed at its very core to serve the interests of democracy, the history of US higher education in particular has always been intertwined with capitalist interests. These capitalist interests seem to be dramatically more visible in the past decade, generating several studies about the commercialization of higher education (Bok 2003), the entrepreneurial university (Mautner 2005), academic capitalism (Slaughter and Leslie 1997), managed education (á la managed health care) (Bousquet 2008), the marketization of higher education (Fairclough 1995), and the postwelfare state university (J. Williams 2006). In fact, however, as Catherine Chaput argues in her book *Inside the Teaching Machine*, "We are not witnessing the corporate takeover of higher education so much as the evolution of an institution constructed through a complex weave of cultural, political, and economic values—none independent of a constantly fluctuating capitalist system" (Chaput 2008, viii). This phase is just the latest in the marriage between higher education and capitalism.

According to Norman Fairclough, the marketization of higher education is simply one (arguably important) example of shifts that have taken place in late-capitalist society more generally (Fairclough 1992, 137–140). In many areas of social life, new domains are increasingly being incorporated into the commodity market (138). Chaput goes further to argue that the very notions of democracy and individual freedom are increasingly equated with "one's ability to access and purchase a variety of commodities" (Chaput 2008, 126). Education, especially postsecondary education, is one such commodity. At the same time, government financial support for higher education has decreased drastically in the last couple of decades. For example, in the 1970s, federal and state financial aid changed from going directly to colleges and universities to going to students (Slaughter 2010, 4). The effect has been that colleges and universities began turning to corporations for both immediate financial backing (e.g., in the form of sponsorships of athletic teams and profit sharing with bookstores) and for more intangible, but no less consequential, profit-motivated models for running the institution.

Put simply, institutions of higher education are increasingly run like corporations, most obviously by competing for the customers/students who have both the money (either as financial aid or out-of-pocket tuition) and the desire to purchase an education. Sheila Slaughter, whose earlier work with Larry L. Leslie on academic capitalism focused on the relationship between corporations and technological and scientific research in universities, argues more recently that a wide variety of practices, services, and organizational structures are now influenced by relationships and shared ideologies with private corporations (Slaughter and Leslie 1997, 2). Decreased state support as well as legislative and legal changes with regard to privatization and deregulation encouraged these shifts in higher education. Chaput argues that the commitment of US universities to participation in the corporate sphere is "increasingly becoming the hegemonic model worldwide," encouraged by supranational associations like the Organization for Economic Cooperation and Development and the World Bank (Chaput 2008, 127).[2]

The corporatization of higher education is a diffuse, complicated, and at times contradictory phenomenon. I focus here on a few elements of this phenomenon most relevant to the issue of retention: labor practices, specifically the reliance on contingent labor; the adoption of certain management practices, especially those influenced by TQM; and the infiltration of promotional culture into higher education. To reiterate, my goal here is to understand the endurance of the discourse of retention despite overwhelming evidence of its ineffectiveness. Retention as an institutional phenomenon is not just a capitulation to what many academics believe are pernicious changes in the culture of higher education. Rather, I argue, retention is an interesting discourse through which to study these changes, in part because it is so complicated, but also because it is potentially a site of resistance to these changes.

RETENTION AND THE CORPORATIZATION OF HIGHER EDUCATION

Concerns about increased reliance on contingent faculty are commonplace in corporatized higher education, and particularly so in writing programs that often rely more on part-time labor than do other units in the college or university. (At my institution, almost 90 percent of first-year writing sections are taught by part-time instructors.) Marc Bousquet's *How the University Works* is an important analysis of this situation and an explanation for the reasons many full-time, tenured, and tenure-track faculty feel helpless but shouldn't. According to Bousquet, the weak job market for PhDs is not an accident but rather "a smoothly functioning new system with its own easily apprehensible logic, premised entirely on the continuous replacement of degree holders with nondegreed labor (or persons with degrees willing to work on unfavorable terms). . . . The academic labor system creates holders of the PhD, but it doesn't have much use for them" (Bousquet 2008, 24–25). Rather, what the system does have a use for is just a few tenured faculty for marketing purposes and a large, flexible, contingent labor pool that provides just-in-time labor/teaching. The academic labor system is mimicking the practices prevalent in corporate settings in an effort to maximize profitability through minimizing labor costs.

A feature of the commonplace of handwringing over contingent labor is the claim that part-time instructors negatively affect the quality of teaching, which in turn negatively affects retention rates. For example, Bousquet himself glances at the issue of retention, conflating it with educational outcomes, in an unsupported claim that "as a result of management's irresponsible staffing practices, more students drop out, take longer to graduate, and fail to acquire essential literacies" (Bousquet 2008, 3). This is an argument that "makes sense"—as commonplaces do—and it is easy to understand the persuasive appeal of such a claim. Advocates for improving faculty benefits and job security, for example a WPA who is arguing for more full-time positions in her program, might appeal to administration's concerns about retention rates by claiming that more full-time instructors will improve these rates.

Such an argument remains entirely framed by management's concern about profit, however: assertions about labor practices' effects on retention rates contend that any profit made through keeping labor costs down is lost through student attrition. Thus, such arguments do not change the terms of the debate at all—profit remains the ultimate end, and the debate simply turns on whether retention or lower labor costs will more easily achieve that end. Moreover, it is a difficult argument to support with empirical research that might persuade administration because of the variety of factors that must be considered when making claims about the relationship between retention and instruction: class size, nature of part-time contracts (union versus nonunion, graduate student instructors versus other part-time instructors, etc.), instructors' credentials, types of courses, student demographics, and so on. It is nearly impossible to isolate the employment status of instructors as a variable in retention.

Furthermore, the relationship between retention and contingent labor in the corporatized university is more complicated than these arguments suggest. I do believe college and

university administration is sincerely concerned about retention, for a variety of reasons. But they also *need* the discourse of
retention—the endless conversations about fluctuating retention and enrollment rates, promotional materials about institutional efforts to improve the rates, and revised job descriptions of higher-level staff to include responsibilities for retention—to justify the overreliance on contingent labor in the
first place. Retention and enrollment data, and the genres that
disseminate the data (Powerpoint charts, formal and informal
conversations, institutional research reports, and so on), verify
the unpredictability of revenue streams. Thus, one reason for
the chronic discourse of retention is to highlight the need to
maintain a flexible labor force and to demand unpaid work
from all faculty.

For example, why must part-time faculty suffer from classes
cut at the last minute? Weak retention numbers. Why must faculty spend more time participating in the new advising effort
or attending summer orientation sessions *without additional compensation?* Such efforts will improve retention. The discourse of
retention is nothing if not complicated, but we see the reductive
power of metonymy at work here. To talk about retention is sincerely to value educational access and success for everyone who
matriculates. But the talk about retention also functions effectively as part of the ideological work necessary to sustain the
economic system emerging in late-capitalist higher education.

Retention functions particularly well in this capacity because
the issue of retention at its most simple is about students' education and success, which are among the most indisputable
shared values of higher education. These values are couched in
warmly compelling language. For example, consider an email
from my institution's president, addressed to the entire college
community in the fall of 2010: "Going forward, we must become
a 'healthier' institution which grows less on ever-increasing
new student enrollment and more on ever-increasing retention
and graduation rates. So what do we do? . . . I am establishing
the recommendations [of a recent task force] as college-wide
principles in order to engage every member of our college

community." And this is the first principle: "The college community will place a spotlight on the new undergraduate student experience seeking to better welcome, integrate, and support our new students." It is difficult for faculty—even, I believe, underpaid and understandably cynical faculty—to easily dismiss efforts to "welcome, integrate, and support" students; for many faculty, students provide the reason to keep working in higher education in the first place, despite the adverse working conditions.

In this email, our president is relying on management practices that derive from movements in the business world, such as Total Quality Management. The infiltration of these management practices into higher education has been neither universal nor uniform; however, Bousquet argues that TQM and related management philosophies have been long institutionalized, "not least by the scene of perpetual retrenchment, in which every year is a year of fiscal crisis, and in which every year sees new pressures on wages, workloads, class sizes, benefits, and autonomy" (Bousquet 2008, 107). And again, the discourse of retention, I assert, communicates this crisis effectively, in part because it does so indirectly.

As part of retention efforts on my campus, everyone was also strongly encouraged to wear special buttons during the first weeks of the semester of fall 2010 to let new students know who we were so they could approach us with questions. There was a button for faculty, one for staff, and one for students, each bearing its own symbol. About the button campaign, the president said in his email, "Our 'button' campaign is a visual reminder for every one of us of our responsibility to support all of our students." We see manifestations of TQM in appeals to team work like this: it is the responsibility of *every one of us* to support students. One consequence of TQM practices is that they distract employees from inequitable labor practices. According to Chaput, "To the extent that faculty members [including contingent faculty, and I might add, staff] succeed as professionals within this framework, they erase the class tensions embedded within their own employment structure. Faculty employees simply become team members who work together to achieve the best customer satisfaction possible" (Chaput 2008, 108). Ultimately, as we see in the email from the president of my institution, what is foregrounded is the sense of shared responsibility, not any specific material practice that will contribute to student success.

In the context of management practices like TQM, the discourse of retention functions not only as part of the persuasive appeal to teamwork—*everybody* is responsible for student success!—but also as a means to assess the effectiveness of one's contribution to the team. One of the most profound effects of the corporatization of higher education, indeed all levels of education, is the increased emphasis on accountability. Retention provides officials with precise data, or at least the illusion of precision, by which to measure the success of programs, departments, individual actors, even whole institutions. Retention numbers act as the point of articulation between the vague area of student experience and the bottom-line economics of the institution in the form of tuition dollars or government funding. Retention as a *preventative* practice is far too complicated to identify in single terms, and yet retention as a *benchmarking* practice can be (and *is*) measured as precisely as a single student's credit hours from semester to semester.

The slippage between retention to signify institutional efforts (like improved instruction, advising, student life, button campaigns) and retention to signify the number of students who return from semester to semester is evident in a recent email from two vice presidents at my college celebrating a rise in retention rates from fall 2010 to spring 2011 compared to the previous year's rates. They quote this year's rate and the precise increase in the number of students and then say, "We have every reason to celebrate this as a community. These numbers reflect the hard work of our college building a community that fosters their passions and pushes them to engage with us on every level—in and outside the classroom." This conflation of retention as the "hard work" of a college and retention as "these numbers" enables administrators to turn the very terms of their persuasive appeals to teamwork into the means by which units must compete for resources: the unit (whether it be a program, department, individual, or even at the state level, institution) with the best retention numbers gets the most of (presumably) limited resources. The discourse of retention, therefore, is not just a mere coincidental extension of the corporatization of higher education but an inextricable cog in the great machine.

As individual units within a college or university compete for internal resources, or institutions compete for tuition dollars and state funding, the object of the competition is students. Enrollment management offices arose alongside, and in conjunction with, the discourse of retention as enrollment managers replaced traditional recruitment and student-services offices. Drawing on the benchmarking practices of TQM and other corporate strategies, enrollment management has played a large role in the transformation of students into consumers (Slaughter 2010, 3–4). As Slaughter notes, the discourse of enrollment management is "painfully obvious in its adaptation of business talk": enrollment managers don't recruit; rather, they market the brand of a particular college or university and try to get customers to buy their "product (future degree)/service (education)" (3). Customer satisfaction is then measured in any number of ways in higher education: through instruments such as the Student Satisfaction Inventory (SSI); through sites such as Rate My Professor and official course evaluations; and through retention numbers.

As students are increasingly seen as customers who must be satisfied, and education is increasingly seen as a commodity that can be branded and marketed like toothpaste, higher education becomes a site for what Norman Fairclough refers to as "promotional culture" (Fairclough 1995, 138–140). Discourse plays an important role in promotional culture (and so, Fairclough argues, must critical discourse analysis play an important role in responding to these ideological shifts) (140). The boundaries among genres are becoming blurrier: press releases sent out from a college are both news and advertisement, course descriptions are used in marketing materials, and so on. Any cursory glance at a college website illustrates the "colonization" of discourse in higher education by promotion (139). On my college's website, following the link for Academics brings you to this text:

> At Columbia College Chicago, academics are so much more than a stack of books and a series of lectures. Your academic program will be your intellectual and creative home: the place where you'll nurture your skills, discover your artistic philosophy, find inspiration, and refuel for further exploration.
>
> You'll learn from active professionals: Pulitzer Prize-winning journalists, Emmy Award-winning producers, and nationally recognized artists, actors, designers, managers, and musicians. You'll get the personal attention you need: Our average class has fewer than 20 students. (Columbia College Chicago n.d.)

Significant here is that on the page ostensibly about the college's academics, it is the student/customer who occupies the subject position in three out of four sentences, and the customer's needs, not the college's academic offerings, are foregrounded. Websites are an easy target for this argument because they are public; therefore, potential students/customers must always be considered. However, the discourse of retention perpetuates this promotional discourse throughout the college because it creates the need to relentlessly advertise the college not just to potential students but to the students already here, who must rechoose to stay each semester. Relentless efforts by Student Life to create a coherent, brand-loyal extracurricular experience are complemented by academic initiatives such as the required first-year seminar, living-learning programs, and even honors programs that are "sold" to current students through promotional discourse—all in the name of retention.

Retention doesn't just perpetuate the promotional culture but has become part of the "package" scrutinized by potential customers. The Student Right-to-Know and Campus Security Act requires colleges and universities to make graduation rates available as part of the larger trend toward increased accountability in higher education. Organizations such as *U.S. News and World Report* help customers with their comparison shopping when they use retention as a key factor in their annual rankings of colleges and universities. In fact, "graduation and retention rates" is one of seven measures in the *U.S. News and World Report* rankings, and it is weighted the same as faculty compensation, faculty credentials, percentage of full-time faculty, student/faculty ratio, and class size *all combined* under the category of "faculty resources" (Morse 2010). I was slightly taken aback recently when a high-school senior I know quoted my college's retention rate to me: her mother had learned to look for these numbers when researching colleges, and they were a key part of their decision-making process about which college the daughter should attend. While the daughter was attracted to the college where I teach for her own reasons, the mother was concerned about the price and the retention rate: the consumer's cost/benefit analysis in today's higher-education market.

It is assumed that the higher the retention rate, the better the product/service. However, Alexander W. Astin reviews data provided by the Cooperative Institutional Research Program (CIRP) derived from surveys of 56,818 students across the country in order to identify those factors that correlate with a tendency to withdraw or persist (Astin 2005–2006, 6). This data measures a wide variety of factors, including, for example, emotional health, popularity, artistic ability, and attendance at religious services, as well as the more predictable factors such as high-school grades, parents' educational level, socioeconomic status, and so forth. (9). Astin's analysis of the CIRP data points to two significant findings: in his words, "an institution's degree completion rate is primarily a reflection of its entering student characteristics, and differences among institutions in their degree completion rates are primarily attributable to differences among their student bodies at the time of entry" (7). In other words, according to Astin's analysis, it is entirely possible for an institution to determine its expected retention rate based only on who the students are *before* beginning college. Astin's argument based on these findings is that "raw" retention rates should not be used by prospective students as a way to choose colleges (presumably the reason they are included in *U.S. News and World Report*'s rankings criteria), nor should they be used by other individuals or organizations, including the government, as a test of an institution's quality.

Rather, according to Astin, one should compare the institution's actual retention rate with the rate of retention one could predict based on the student body's entry characteristics. An institution that enrolls students who are at a greater risk of dropping out, as determined by their entry characteristics, but that actually keeps more students than predicted is doing a better job than another institution that loses more students than it should (again, as determined by entry characteristics) (Astin 2005–2006, 11). Astin anticipates the insidious corollary of his findings, and he is particularly concerned with state governments that use raw retention rates as a measure of accountability to determine funding: "The danger of such state policies is that they discourage institutions from enrolling relatively poorly prepared students in order to maximize their raw retention rates" (15).

Astin's analysis indicates that understanding retention is much more complicated than the average consumer appreciates. But average consumers have learned to approach higher education in the same way they approach other products and services, looking not for information, necessarily, but for reasons to be persuaded to purchase the commodity. We see in retention rates an example of, in Fairclough's terms, "a widespread instrumentalization of discursive practices, involving the subordination of meaning to, and the manipulation of meaning for, instrumental effect" (Fairclough 1995, 139). To cite other examples: faculty bios are written not (just) to provide information about credentials and scholarly interests but to promote the college, and the student handbook is written not (just) to provide information about resources but to promote the college. Federal law mandates that information about retention be made available, but in the context of the corporatization of higher education, students who identify as consumers will read such information as part of the larger promotional culture in which it is embedded. The complicated, multifaceted meaning of *retention rate* becomes subordinate to the practices of potential consumers.

Colleges and universities know this and participate in subordinating and manipulating the meaning of *retention* to their promotional and competitive needs. I illustrate this point in the next section as part of a closer analysis of the discourse of retention as it circulates locally at my own institution.

RETENTION: AN ANALYSIS OF A KEYWORD

The point of the previous discussion is to work toward an understanding of the reasons we're still talking about retention, but, in fact, when we consider all the research, all the programs and policies and new hires put in place, all the statistics and data and charts, all the college-wide conversations about retention, we see none of it has drastically changed retention rates nationally. At individual institutions like my own, whose retention rates have risen slightly over the last several years, it is extremely difficult to determine whether the intentional efforts of the institution have done anything to change retention rates, or whether the rates are affected by changes in the size, demographics, and educational background of the entering student body, as Astin's analysis maintains. My argument above is that the discourse of retention cannot be understood as an isolated phenomenon; rather, retention is deeply integrated into the social context of the corporatization of higher education in many ways.

In his introduction to *Keywords*, Raymond Williams cautions that

> the problem of meaning can never be wholly dissolved into context. It is true that no word ever finally stands on its own, since it is always an element in the social process of language, and its uses depend on complex and (though variably) systematic properties of language itself. Yet it can still be useful to pick out certain words, of an especially problematical kind, and to consider, for the moment, their own internal developments and structures. (R. Williams 1983, 22–23)

If my discussion above dissolves retention into context, the analysis that follows studies the "internal developments and structures" of this keyword.

Specifically, I'm interested here in how the discourse of retention, manifested in textual instances of the word itself, has changed in recent years. Fairclough argues that discursive change "leaves traces in texts" that can be identified (Fairclough 1992, 97). These traces are not merely textual remnants of social changes, however; changes in the way we use a word like *retention* can contribute to social changes like those I discuss above. I analyze the self-studies produced by my college as part of the accreditation process through the Higher Learning Commission of the North Central Association of Colleges and Schools. Studying these documents is useful for my purposes because these two documents were written ten years apart, in 1999 and 2009, following the cycle of re-accreditation, so they provide a contrast across time even as they maintain the same primary audience, same writing process, and same purpose.[3] Moreover, they were collaboratively drafted by constituents from across the college as part of an exercise in self-reflection, so they represent the collective understanding of the state of the college; however, at the same time, they are very much administrative documents as opposed to documents situated within the pedagogical or student life functions of the college. (I was on the very large committee that participated in the research and writing of the 2009 self-study; much of the work we did was significantly revised by the vice president overseeing the re-accreditation process, who was responsible for compiling the work of the various subcommittees.)

As I note in chapter 1, the intervening decade between the 1999 and 2009 self-studies saw a drastic increase in the amount of scholarship produced on the topic of retention. There were as many as 35 percent more dissertations cataloged in Dissertation Abstracts about retention in this decade than in the previous ten years. And my own project has been developed in response to what I've experienced as a real intensification of the discourse of retention in my workplace, both at my current institution and at the university where I taught previously: more people have been talking about retention in both casual and official contexts more often, more people have been hired and more programs have been revised or instituted in the name of retention, and data on retention have been circulated more frequently. As my introduction discusses, in nonacademic settings, the topic of retention has been raised more frequently in news media and political contexts. Even casually among friends and neighbors, people who are generally ambivalent about what I do for a living have something to say about this project when it comes up.

As I began this analysis of the two self-studies, then, I expected that, regardless of what else I would find, at the very least there would be more instances of the word *retention* in the 2009 document than in the 1999 self-study, that the intensification of the discourse would be reflected in the quantity of references to this keyword. To my surprise, this was not the case. In the 1999 self-study, there was an eleven-page section titled "Undergraduate Retention and Graduation" in addition to many, many more references to retention throughout the document, but in the entire 2009 self-study report, there were only twenty-nine instances of the word *retention*; three of those instances referred to faculty retention (the issue of hiring and retaining faculty), so essentially there were twenty-six references to undergraduate retention in the 2009 self-study. My analysis turned to the function and signification of this keyword in these documents: Does the word *mean* the same thing in both, and to what extent has discursive change left traces in these texts? For the purposes of this analysis, I compared the twenty-six references to student retention in the 2009 self-study with the eleven-page essay in the 1999 self-study.

The most noticeable shift in usage, the one symptomatic of the larger discursive changes occurring in the intervening decade between the two documents, is the increased use of retention as a stand-alone concept in the 2009 document, where the keyword appears as an unmodified noun with no object or prepositional phrase following it. So, for example, in the 2009 self-study, the following are typical instances of retention:

> EX. 1: The college created the Division of Student Affairs, established a partnership between Student Affairs and Academic

Affairs, and committed to improving *retention* and student-centeredness. (Columbia College Chicago 2010b, 8)

and

EX. 2: Columbia is also building a data warehouse to create easy access to standardized data about enrollment, *retention*, diversity, etc. (51; italics added)

In the 1999 self-study, by contrast, the concept of retention is more likely to appear in phrases such as:

EX. 3: Over the course of the last six years, Columbia has substantially redefined institutional responsibility for *retaining* students. (Columbia College Chicago 2010a, 213; italics added)

and

EX. 4: Columbia's undergraduate programs *retain* and graduate lower than the average percent of students at other open admissions colleges. (216; italics added)

In examples 1 and 2, the term *retention* has swallowed the surrounding modifiers and objects that appear in examples 3 and 4, and the action of retaining students is backgrounded. This shift shares some of the implications of nominalization: according to Fairclough, "Nominalization is the conversion of processes into nominals, which has the effect of backgrounding the process itself—its tense and modality are not indicated—and usually not specifying its participants, so that who is doing what to whom is left implicit" (Fairclough 1992, 179). In the case of retention in these two documents, the process by which the college works to help students succeed, presumably an active process that seriously affects the human actors involved, becomes an abstract concept. This shift is further highlighted in the differences in content between examples 2 and 3: in example 2 from 2009, the sentence is about building a "data warehouse" to "standardize data," whereas in example 3 from 1999, the sentence foregrounds Columbia's responsibility for student success.

What is striking about this shift is how pervasive it is: in the 2009 self-study, *retention* appears in ten of the twenty-six instances as a stand-alone, unmodified concept; in the 1999 self-study, four of the first twenty-six instances of *retention* in the section titled "Undergraduate Retention and Graduation" appear this way, suggesting that the occurrence of this usage more than doubles in ten years. There is what I think of as an isolation and ossification of the concept of retention; the term still refers to the problem of students leaving before graduation and efforts to address this problem, but the dynamic nature of this problem becomes suppressed.

Further evidence of this isolation and ossification is apparent in an analysis of the markers of intertextuality in the two documents. The 1999 self-study contains more, and more clearly marked, instances of intertextuality than the 2009 self-study. In other words, reading the 1999 self-study, it is easier to see the other texts—conversations, documents, and so forth—that the authors drew on during the production process, whereas in the 2009 self-study, there are very few markers of intertextuality surrounding the discussion of retention. The effect of this difference is explained by Fairclough:

> If the surface of a text may be multiply determined by the various other texts which go into its composition, then elements of that textual surface may not be clearly placed in relation to the text's intertextual network, and their meaning may be ambivalent; different meanings may coexist, and it may not be possible to determine 'the' meaning. (Fairclough 1992, 105).

So, in a document like the 1999 self-study, which is "multiply determined by the various other texts which go into its composition," there is room for a variety of meanings surrounding the concept of retention, and the movement among those meanings creates a more dynamic discourse. When these markers are absent, as in the 2009 self-study, there is a greater reliance on *the* single meaning, which, as I say above, becomes ossified, less available to contradictory or multiple voices.

The 1999 self-study is interesting because of the variety of types of texts evident in its composition: from other administrative documents produced by the college to voices of faculty and staff to research and scholarship on retention. In the first couple of paragraphs of the eleven-page section titled "Undergraduate Retention and Graduation," the document contains references to an address by the president of the college calling for "renewed college wide efforts to improve retention and graduation rates"; to the college's strategic vision statement, which connects the open enrollment policy of the college to the challenge of retention; and to faculty and staff, one an indirect quote of faculty and staff "who expressed very eloquently their unease with the number of students who dropped out before completing their degrees" and a substantial direct quote of a participant at a town meeting who urged institutional, departmental, and individual faculty commitment to respond to students who are not doing well (Columbia College Chicago 2010a, 213–14). Each of these references open up the meaning of retention so that in the short space of these two paragraphs, *retention* comes to encompass a president's charge, the institutional efforts to help students stick around, the rise in rates these efforts have yielded, the mission-driven imperative of graduating as many students as possible, the feelings of faculty and staff who work with students who subsequently drop out, and the sense of responsibility on several levels. The discourse here is multifaceted and variable in a way that it is not in the 2009 self-study.

Even beyond these first couple of paragraphs, throughout the section "Undergraduate Retention and Graduation" in the 1999 self-study, there is evidence of intertextuality and the mix of styles this entails. Although both documents are official representations of the college's response to the problem of retention, the 1999 self-study manifests the complex nature of the problem by drawing on both local lore and published scholarship. For example, the study introduces a list of facts about retention at Columbia this way: "The things the College knows for certain so far are common sense and useful for setting retention strategies" (Columbia College Chicago 2010a, 217), asserting the value of common sense and local knowledge about the issue. (The use of the word *things* also marks a more casual style, which is consistent with the reference to common sense.) Even when the 1999 self-study does refer to official scholarship, it is tied to local knowledge. For example:

These findings [refers to local research], which are consistent with much of the current literature about causes of attrition and strategies for retention, reflect one of the challenges of Columbia's phenomenal growth. (218)

and

In devising the goals and strategies which appear in *Laying the Foundation* [the strategic vision statement], the College drew heavily on the work of Vincent Tinto and other recent research on student success in college. (219)

This mix of local and national research presents a heterogeneous understanding of retention that is more open to multiple responses.

Absent in the 2009 self-study, the references to other texts and discourses I notice in the 1999 self-study represent retention as a multifaceted and variable issue. This representation is further developed through references to other realms of human experience such as failure and morality that intersect with the issue of retention. For example, the word *attrition*—meaning the loss of students, or the failure of retention efforts—does not appear in the 2009 self-study, but the 1999 self-study refers to attrition throughout the eleven-page section, as well as to "students who dropped out" (Columbia College Chicago 2010a, 214) and groups who "leave without graduating" (214). The 1999 self-study states plainly that Columbia's "undergraduate retention and graduation rates are lower than they should be," and in the next sentence refers back to this assertion as "the problem" (rather than, say, "the challenge" or the more neutral "the issue") (223). This acknowledgment of deficiency is completely absent in the 2009 self-study. Likewise, the 2009 self-study does not use the words *persist* or *persistence* anywhere—terms that frame the issue of retention from the perspective of individual students: persistence refers to the student's movement through college, whereas retention refers to the institution's ability to keep students enrolled. The consistent use of *retention* in the 2009 self-study, and the absence of *attrition* or *persistence*, frame the issue entirely from the single perspective of institutional success. Perhaps most troubling in the 2009 self-study is the absence of references to the moral nature of retention. In the 1999 self-study, the first paragraph frames the commitment to student success as "both the smart and the moral thing to do" (213).

The lack of interdiscursivity and manifest intertextuality in the 2009 self-study, coupled with the consistent use of *retention* as an unmodified nominalization, create the sense that *retention* has a single, official meaning. The dynamic nature of the problem of retention is backgrounded in favor of an ossified, isolated, and internally consistent concept. The methodology of critical discourse analysis allows for an appreciation of how these textual details both reflect and contribute to the social changes I discuss earlier in the chapter. Bousquet argues that "higher education administration pervasively and self-consciously seeks control of the institution by seeking to retool the values, practices, and sense of institutional reality that comprise faculty and student culture" (Bousquet 2008, 12). While I am not in a position to determine how self-consciously the administration of my college has taken control of the discourse of retention, I do see the changes in this discourse represented in these self-studies as both reflecting and constructing an approach to retention more in line with the corporatization of higher education.

A single, consistent referent is more conducive to the promotional culture that pervades higher education, for example. Although both documents were written for the same audience and purpose, there is clearly a sense in the 2009 self-study that the college is deliberately promoting itself as much as, or more than, it is studying itself. So, rather than allowing for faculty and staff's concerns about student dropouts, or admitting the problem of attrition, as the 1999 self-study does, the overwhelmingly dominant impression of retention in the 2009 self-study is positive: as a singular, definitive concept, it is predictably "improving" and "increasing" and services are "being enhanced."

Moreover, the 2009 self-study more consistently refers to concepts that come from managerial discourse, such as "entering student profile" (Columbia College Chicago 2010b, 8), "student satisfaction ratings" (10), "enrollment priorities" (25), "admissions yields" (78), and so on. None of these phrases appears in the 1999 self-study. It is worth noting, too, that the 2009 self-study does not mark these rare moments of intertextuality in obvious ways—while a reader like me recognizes these terms as borrowed from other discourses, there are no signal phrases such as those that appear in the 1999 self-study. Thus, on the surface, the tenor of the retention discourse in the 2009 self-study is more monovocal, one that is consistent with the managerial discourse that dominates other genres circulating at the college.

Where I expected an increase in the quantity of discussion of retention from 1999 to 2009, I found instead an increase in the stability of the keyword itself, lending itself to more predictably contribute to the "values, practices, and sense of institutional reality" that serve administrative tendencies toward the corporatization of higher education generally, and my college specifically. It appears that the lengthier, more involved discussion in the 1999 self-study allowed for more perspectives, contradictory impulses, and multiple significations. The discourse of retention in the 2009 self-study is more effective at meeting the needs of the administration because it is so monotonous.

RETENTION AND RESISTANCE

While the changes in the discourse of retention over the ten years between the two self-studies are favorable to the corporatization of higher education, Fairclough reminds us that "it is important to avoid an image of discursive change as a unilinear, top-down process: there is struggle over the structuring of texts and orders of discourse and people may resist or appropriate changes coming from above, as well as merely go along with them" (Fairclough 1992, 9). The multiple, and at times contradictory, perspectives on the issue of retention evident in the 1999 self-study have not disappeared from campus even though they aren't obvious in the 2009 self-study. Just as on any other campus in the United States, it is difficult to ignore the social changes surrounding higher education at Columbia College, and the topic of retention is clearly an important feature of those changes. However, although the struggle over and resistance to the issue of retention may not be evident in the surface-level features of the text of the 2009 self-study, every faculty and staff member is not walking around, zombie-like, spouting data about student satisfaction ratings and admissions yields.

Moreover, as Chaput reminds us, the trends toward the corporatization of higher education do not represent a new era in higher education but a continuation of elements that have been intrinsic to higher education in the Unites States since the beginning:

> Though it is certainly tempting to assume that recent discussion over how universities function in service to global capitalism stems from a fundamental change in the university's relationship to society, it is important to remember that this university system emerged by, through, and in service to a capitalist political economy that unevenly combines corporate, state, and civic interests. (Chaput 2008, 119)

Therefore, she argues, nostalgic appeals for a return to "the purity of our past democratic mission" will inevitably fail because they ignore the very nature of the institution (120). The same is true for the issue of retention: there was no golden age when every student who enrolled in college subsequently graduated four years later. The persistent push toward improving retention rates, and the lamentation that ensues when we fail to do so, always seems to assume that we're abandoning previously held ideals. This simply isn't the case: just as higher education in the United States has always been intimately knotted up with capitalism, higher education has always been structured on the premise that not everyone will earn a degree. Admissions practices aren't the only way students have been excluded from completing a college education: students have always left before graduation for the myriad reasons they still leave (academic performance, mental and physical illnesses, family obligations, financial struggles, etc.).

In fact, one of the reasons retention is such a fascinating discourse is that it contains within it the impulses I describe in this chapter toward metonymically reducing the complicated process of education down to the bottom line, the number of credit hours for which tuition can be charged. At the same time, this discourse contains the complicated reasons students might leave, an instructor's uncomfortable feelings when working with a student who is failing or who decides to leave, the questions about our responsibilities to educate all who enroll, and the ethical struggles over the severe limits to our abilities to do so—some limits of our own making, others we have no control over. When we pause, and push back at the numbers, we see metonymy breaking down.

When the discourse on retention becomes monovocal, and the term itself is reduced to an agentless nominalization that refers to rates and policies instead of teachers and students, the most important element of the discourse we lose is students' stories. Part of my project here is to resist this trend, to reinsert into this discourse the more complicated, challenging questions about our goals and responsibilities and our struggles to meet them. The discourse of retention does contain within it our very best intentions to educate, the loftiest ideals for a flourishing democracy. And the discourse of retention is also about the students who do leave—perhaps to return later, perhaps not. Cesar's story is about all of this.

Because he was enrolled in one of my courses each semester of his first year of college and attended my class and office hours regularly, and because he was a participant in the Student Faculty Partnership for Success program, which I had designed and coordinated specifically to support students like Cesar, I was responsible for a good deal of his experience of higher education. I was trying to do my part to boost my college's retention rate: I was a team player. Of course, I wasn't just taking orders from my college president. I was teaching first-year writing as best I could.

And honestly, I just really, really like Cesar. He wrote and talked a lot about his changing attitudes, his many lives. He changed course after getting out of a gang in elementary school (and getting shot at for doing so). He changed after almost joining another gang in the new school he moved to in order to escape the first gang. He changed again his junior year in high school when he decided to rise above the rules that governed the social lives of his classmates, and again his senior year when he decided to start thinking about college. *Another new life. Another life that I got,* he said when I quipped about how much change he'd been through. I asked him how important it was to him that he graduate from college. He replied, *I'll be actually the first one in my family to graduate from college, show that even if you're a gangbanger or you're anything at all, you could still succeed in life with anything. It's within yourself.* College seemed to represent the possibility of another moment of transformation, not just for him, but for his family and for others. This is the narrative that motivated me to do what I could for Cesar: nothing else in the discourse of retention, not the college president's exhortations to teamwork, not the threat of weakening budgets, not even my own research held more persuasive power than the hope that an incredibly bright, hard-working student would achieve what he set out to achieve.

In his writing and in our conversations, I heard a tension between his past and his future, between his Latino family and the white institution of higher education, between the hope of a college degree and the struggle that surrounded his efforts to obtain one. The first major essay he wrote in my class begins, "Being a Latino can sometimes be hard in America. . . . In my family my father says we should be what we are meant to be, meaning that America has the decision of who we will be in the future. I don't think that way. Sometimes I might but that's not my answer to everything." This passage seems to turn on the two instances of "sometimes": sometimes being a Latino is hard, sometimes he agrees with his father that America has assigned places for immigrants. But sometimes he doesn't think that way. The title of this piece is "I Made It": the use of the past tense belies the indeterminacy of this passage and the *in media res* quality of the first line, "Being a Latino . . . "

His career goal was to be in the music business, to manage artists. (He is extremely driven and already had some success in the music business when he first enrolled in college.) But during the semesters he was in my courses, he talked often about a personal goal to help kids leave gangs or prevent them from joining in the first place. The final assignment in Cesar's first-semester writing class required that students think carefully about audience. Drawing on Susan Wells, I talked to the students about "constructing a responsive public" for the writing they do (Wells 1996, 329). The time we spent on Wells's ideas did not do her argument justice, but most of the students, at least, understood that the circulation of texts in our society is severely constrained and that "our public sphere is attenuated, fragmented, and colonized," that for writers, there are no easy, ready-made audiences (329).

Upon receiving the assignment, Cesar called a school principal and asked her if he could speak to an assembly of students about stopping and preventing gang violence. And just like that, he had an audience. He reported in class, "I talked to the principal, and I'm meeting with her next week." And then, "I met with her and we scheduled the assembly for November 24. Is it okay if I miss class that day, because it's on the West Side and I don't know if I'll make it back in time?" He recruited a classmate to join him. Then, "The assembly got postponed. It's on December 2." And finally, "We did it. It went great." Reflecting on the project, Cesar wrote, "To create an audience you have to know who the audience will be. . . . My audience was Elementary School Students. The audience is the most important thing; you want someone to hear what you're going to say." He continued: "What have I learned in writing? Allot [I] am not the best writer, but I have learned through my reading I have spoken out. That's why writing is part of a revolution."

At the time he was writing this, I knew he was registered for classes the next semester, including my Writing and Rhetoric II class, a research-writing course. However, I also knew that as much as he wanted to be in college, he wasn't unconditionally confident that he would be able to persist. In an interview right around this time, at the end of the first semester, I asked him, "Where do you see yourself two years from now?" His reply betrays this lack of confidence: *I see myself still working and probably still at school. I hope so.* I also knew he struggled financially, trying to juggle work, private loans, Stafford loans, and his father's ambivalence about Cesar attending college. (At one low point in the semester, Cesar moved out of his parents' home when he found out his father had sent all the money Cesar had saved to family in Mexico, possibly as much as $700, money Cesar was planning on using to pay tuition.)

In the second semester, Cesar continued his work on preventing gang violence. His research project was centered on how to prevent kids from joining gangs or how to help kids leave once they've joined. Like the work he did to plan and execute his talk to the elementary students the previous semester, much of the research he did for this project seemed to fall outside the scope of my class. He got a job with a local organization that specialized in gang intervention and participated in a program that took young kids to the prison and the morgue to show them the likely consequences of gang life. He talked to individuals and met with their families. In his final paper, he told the story of a friend who was killed in gang violence and the story of others who were trying to get out. Attached to the research paper was a flier for a march and rally he was helping to plan, Ending the Cycle of Violence, scheduled for the first weekend after the semester ended. He also attached a one-page, handwritten letter from one of the kids he helped. In it, the kid wrote, "I promise I will not hang out with the bad people you know dem gangbangers. I will let you know what school I will transfer to. I was lucky to be one of the students you helped."

Cesar left college after his first year. There was nothing I could do; at least I don't think there was anything I could do. I got an email from him toward the end of summer letting me know that his dad lost his job and he wouldn't be returning. I took this news personally; I felt the disappointment physically. I am critical of the discourse of retention as it circulates on my college campus and increasingly cynical about the claim that the tremendous amount of time and energy and money we're spending on improving the retention rate will have any positive effects, but at the same time I really wish Cesar could have enrolled for another year, and then two more, and graduate with a degree in music business. At least I think this is what I wish—if graduation is what would be best for him.

When the discourse of retention gets reduced to a monovocal, institutionalized refrain about credit hours and enrollment trends, we are ignoring the stories of students like Cesar and the struggles of instructors like me who are invested personally and professionally in how these stories turn out. When we put on buttons or tout a new advising program, we are ignoring the much more difficult questions about what we should be doing for students like Cesar, how we can best serve him *as a student,* not as a potential dip in the retention rate.

I argue at the beginning of this chapter that the discourse of retention is both a product of broader social changes surrounding higher education and as a site of tension within, or evidence of ambivalence about, if not resistance to, these changes. The resistance can come when we focus our conversations about retention on students like Cesar and ask the hard questions. What role should my course play in the educational experience of a student like Cesar? What is the value of my course for Cesar if he never graduates? One-fourth of the money he spent on the first year of college paid for the classes he took with me. So how do I want Cesar to respond to the question I posed: What did you learn about writing? Knowing what I know about Cesar and about the statistical chances that he may not graduate, what is the right answer to that question? "Writing is part of a revolution," he tells me.

Ultimately, we cannot prevent all students from dropping out. Neither can we predict who will graduate and who won't. Research on retention and the experiences of students who leave remind us that the cost of higher education is much higher for students who do not earn a degree, an issue I discuss at greater length in the next chapter. And yet, if the exchange value of our courses fluctuates from student to student, is there still a way for us to talk about the value of our courses for all of our students, including those who leave? Ultimately, the real benefit of the discourse of retention comes from asking the question, what is my responsibility to Cesar?

NOTES

1. Admittedly, CDA has not been widely recognized by my colleagues in composition and rhetoric, but that may be changing: a recent conference at the University of Utah, which brought together North and South American scholars who use CDA, was initiated and coordinated by Thomas Huckin, a leading figure in our field. I have long found CDA to be extremely compatible with—and in fact, very instructive for—my work in composition studies and rhetoric, and I feel confident that readers who identify as rhetoricians or compositionists will feel comfortable with the vocabulary here.

2. Fairclough's and Andrea Mayr's work on British institutions indicate that Chaput is correct, at least in that country (see Fairclough 1995, 130–66; Mayr 2008, 26–45).

3. The documents are listed in the references under the author Columbia College Chicago (2010a, 2010b), with the titles "1998/1999 Columbia College Self Study Report: Volume One" and "HLC/NCA Self-Study Report Spring 2009," respectively.

3
THE POSSIBILITY OF FAILURE

If you do a search in Amazon for books with the keyword *failure*, the vast majority of titles are about success: *The Power of Failure: 27 Ways to Turn Life's Setbacks into Success*; *Famous Failures: Hundreds of Hot Shots Who Got Rejected, Flunked Out, Worked Lousy Jobs, Goofed Up, or Did Time in Jail Before Becoming a Phenomenal Success*; *Success Through Failure*; *Great Failures of the Extremely Successful*; *Failure: The Back Door to Success*. In other words, if you went by nothing other than these titles, you would think it a great stroke of luck if you failed tremendously at something. And we love the stories of people like Bill Gates, who dropped out of college, or Albert Einstein, who failed his entrance exams to the Zurich Polytechnic, because we know these stories end with phenomenal success (Gladwell 2008, 50; Isaacson 2007, 25). We want to imagine similar endings to the stories of Cesar and Helen, who left the college where I met them after just a semester or two. But no matter how many self-help books tell us that, in the words of another title listed on Amazon, *The Road to Success is Paved with Failure*, the fact of the matter is that failure is much more complicated and a lot less auspicious than we'd like to believe.

The problem of failure is at the murky center of the issue of student retention at American colleges and universities. Both in retention literature and in the literature of composition studies, when we talk about students who are "at risk," we are talking about students who are at risk *for failure*. As the omission of *failure* in the phrase *at risk* suggests, rarely is failure openly or easily discussed; rather, failure occurs in the shadows of our professional discourse. The shadows sometimes lead us to see things that aren't there and prevent us from seeing things that are. When students leave, our retention discourse tends to ascribe failure *to the students*, regardless of the circumstances of their

DOI: 10.7330/9780874219319.c003

leaving. Some students transfer to another institution, some "stop out" (leave for a couple of semesters or years, but return to earn the degree), and some do in fact leave for good—and for many students, these are not necessarily failure situations. However, while students may not experience leaving as failure, a student who leaves is always an indication of failure for the institution. And even though students' leaving is typically understood as a financial failure in the form of lost revenue, when students leave, teachers and institutions must confront our own failures at a deeper level, too: it is impossible to educate students who are not there. We simply cannot achieve our pedagogical goals or institutional missions when students leave.

As I argue in the previous chapters, despite the increasing intensity of the discourse of retention on our college campuses, we may never be able to solve the problem of student dropouts, or attrition more generally; however, this discourse can still be useful to us if we come closer to defining for ourselves what our goals as teachers and as institutions ought to be—and this, I argue, should be at the center of our focus on retention. Thus, this chapter is about failure, but my aim is to deflect the issue of retention away from student failure to a reconsideration of our own failures as faculty and institutions and our own complicity in the rhetoric of failure that surrounds the individual student's decision to leave an institution before graduation.

First, the etymology of failure, the history of the concept of failure in the financial world that I discuss in the next couple of sections, connects the issue of retention to the problem of student debt and also begins to explain why we tend to ascribe failure to an individual rather than to an institution or society as a whole. Then I return to the discourse of retention to discuss how the seminal work of retention scholar Vincent Tinto reinforces the emphasis on the individual, effectively impeding the development of more sustaining and systemic means of addressing attrition. Finally, I make connections between retention scholarship and scholarship in the fields of basic writing and disability studies in order to make the argument that the real failure in all of these areas is our own failure of imagination, our inability to envision an institution of higher education that can successfully educate every student who sits in our classrooms, a radically inclusive institution that may, ironically, include students who leave.

FAILURE: FROM INCIDENT TO IDENTITY

When Barack Obama spoke to the nation for the first time as our president, he admitted that he took the oath of office "amidst gathering clouds and raging storms" (Obama 2009b). On the occasion of Obama's inaugural address, the country was elated that we had just elected our first African American president, but we were also reeling from the preceding weeks of watching the nation's economic implosion. We were beginning to realize that the banks collapsing around us were no longer lending money for college tuition, mortgages, or small business expansion, and that our neighbors—if not ourselves—were not going to escape unscathed.

"That we are in the midst of a crisis is now well understood," President Obama stated. Relevant here is how Obama framed the crisis: it is, he said, "a consequence of greed and irresponsibility on the part of some but also our collective failure to make hard choices and prepare the nation for a new age" (Obama 2009b). In his first address to joint session of Congress a month later, he was more pointed in asserting that every individual and family bore some personal responsibility for the problems we faced:

> Now if we're honest with ourselves, we'll admit that for too long, we have not always met these responsibilities—as a government or as a people. . . . In other words, we have lived through an era where too often, short-term gains were prized over long-term prosperity; where we failed to look beyond the next payment, the next quarter, or the next election. A surplus became an excuse to transfer wealth to the wealthy instead of an opportunity to invest in our future. Regulations were gutted for the sake of a quick profit at the expense of a healthy market. People bought homes they knew they couldn't afford from banks and lenders who pushed those bad loans anyway. (Obama 2009a)

Individualizing failure, as Obama's rhetoric does—*each one of us* has failed to meet responsibilities—is commensurate with the larger discourse of individual drive and ambition. In fact, as historian Scott A. Sandage argues in *Born Losers*, "Failure is not the dark side of the American Dream; it is the foundation of it" (Sandage 2005, 278). In order to believe that individuals can pull themselves up by their bootstraps, we have to believe that it is possible for individuals to fail to do so (18). Rhetorician Victor Villanueva, writing about his own bootstraps experience, makes a similar point: "He has made it by the bootstraps: GED to PhD—an American success story. But he knows that for most like him, the bootstraps break before the boots are on, that too many have no boots" (Villanueva 1993, xiv).

The bootstraps myth runs very deep in our culture, in part because we believe that the ability to succeed (despite the real possibility of failure) comes from deep in our character; it is part of our very moral fiber. To dismiss the bootstraps myth as myth is to dismiss some of our fundamental beliefs about virtue. We see this in Obama's Inaugural Address:

> Greatness is never a given. It must be earned. Our journey has never been one of shortcuts or settling for less. It has not been the path for the faint-hearted, for those who prefer leisure over work, or seek only pleasures of riches and fame. Rather it has been the risk-takers, the doers, the makers of things. (Obama 2009b)

Those who have succeeded, and who have made America great, Obama proclaims, do not possess the dishonorable traits of laziness or cowardice or gluttony. Those who succeed are a special kind of people. In *Outliers: The Story of Success*, Malcolm Gladwell explores this belief that successful people are exceptional, unique:

> What is the question we always ask about the successful? We want to know what they're *like*—what kind of personalities they have, or how intelligent they are, or what kind of lifestyles they have, or what special talents they might have been born with. And we assume that it is those personal qualities that explain how that individual reached the top. (Gladwell 2008, 18)

Outliers spent over a year on the *New York Times* bestseller list, in part, I'm assuming, because many buyers thought Gladwell would identify these traits and explain how to achieve them (much like all those books that turn up on Amazon with a search for *failure*).

However, Gladwell's argument is that we're wrong—success is not about personality traits and virtue. Rather, success is about chance and circumstances like birthdays. (He makes a very compelling case that the success of the richest business people in America—Rockefeller, Carnegie, J.P. Morgan, for example—and the success of pro hockey and pro baseball players, has more to do with when they were born than with any special personality trait or talent.) Gladwell argues that "because we so profoundly personalize success, we miss opportunities to lift others onto the top rung. We make rules that frustrate achievement. We prematurely write off people as failures. We are too much in awe of those who succeed and far too dismissive of those who fail" (Gladwell 2008, 32–33). Gladwell's argument about our contemporary beliefs about success and failure echoes Sandage's history of failure in the nineteenth century. Sandage argues that in the nineteenth century, Americans "looked upon failure as a 'moral sieve' that trapped the loafer and passed the true man through. Such ideologies fixed blame squarely on individual faults, not extenuating circumstances" (Sandage 2005, 17).

But Americans didn't always believe this way. Sandage argues that this ideology was born in the nineteenth century. Prior to that, sin was a greater concern than losing money. *Failure* in the beginning of the nineteenth century was a term applied only to business events, a synonym for *breaking* (Sandage 2005, 11). By the middle of the nineteenth century, the term *failure* could refer to an individual but remained within the discourse of business. Sandage quotes the *Merchants' and Bankers' Almanac,* published in 1861, which defined *failure* as "the general term applied to an individual or concern that has become bankrupt" (qtd. on 12). But in this one term, we see the insinuation of capitalism into the most intimate areas of human life as this term for financial ruin became increasingly used to refer to moral ruin until we no longer see it as a figure of speech. It is now, in Sandage's words, "the language of business applied to the soul" (5).

Failure is no longer an incident, but an identity (Sandage 2005, 10–11). Where once a person first "broke" in business and therefore earned the title of failure, now we are willing to assume that it is a moral failure that leads to financial ruin. When Obama addressed our national economic crisis, he could blame our failure, but not limit it to our failures in business; rather it is our "failure to make hard choices" that preceded the financial ruin, our failures of character. Jeffrey Williams brings this closer to home in "The Pedagogy of Debt." He argues that "in the quintessentially middle class precincts of academe, people don't descend to talk about bread basket issues like salary and debt. It's crass, like clipping coupons. And it is shameful, reflecting your failing" (J. Williams 2006, 156). We don't like to talk about debt, our own or our students', in part because financial failings are conflated with moral failings. But by avoiding the issue of debt, we are avoiding a central experience in most of our students' lives, and in the context of retention, this issue is key. How do our beliefs about failure—shaped as they are by the ideology that arose in the nineteenth century—influence our attitudes toward students who leave? And what are our responsibilities to our students, considering the role that higher education plays in an individual's lifetime financial picture?

STUDENTS GOING BROKE: FAILING IN THE BUSINESS OF HIGHER EDUCATION

It is generally assumed that a college degree is a good investment. At my institution's graduation in spring 2009, the president of the college used this very phrase, "a good investment," to describe the degrees he was awarding that day. It was like trying to throw a handful of peanuts at the stampeding elephant in the room: one of the worst job markets in recent history. But generally, the facts and figures support the assumption that, in the long run, a college degree is worth the financial burden. There are a number of ways to measure the value of a college degree—average income, median income, lifetime earnings, benefits to one's health and to one's children, and so on—but by all measures, it appears far better to have a college degree than not. For example, according to one analysis, in 2000, the average earnings for people twenty years or older with a bachelor's degree or higher was $65,000, while those in the same age group with just a high-school diploma earned on average $33,000 (Weinberg 2004, 3). Moreover, the benefits of a college degree are realized by people across races and ethnicities and by people of all genders (Baum and Ma 2007).

While a college degree typically tends to ensure some measure of financial well-being that a high-school diploma does not, usually the benefits of a college degree are set against the rising cost of tuition and other expenses. And we speak of tuition as an investment, and wonder about the risks associated with it, because of the increasing amount of debt assumed by most families who send a family member to college. A report commissioned by the US Department of Education in 2006, titled "A Test of Leadership: Charting the Future of U.S. Higher Education," found that not only is the cost of higher education outpacing inflation and family income, but that the current financial aid structure is completely ineffective at meeting these challenges (U.S. Department of Education 2006, 10). The authors of the report argue that the entire financial aid system "is confusing, complex, inefficient, duplicative, and frequently does not direct aid to students who truly need it" (12). They recommend that the system be completely restructured (19).

Especially in the current financial environment, it is increasingly common to hear people ask, as one author put it, "Are college loans worth the risk?" (O'Toole 2006, 26). There is talk of a "crisis" of student debt: students won't seek out lower-paying careers in nonprofits or ministry or teaching, they'll put off marriage, they'll drown in debt. And while there is not much actual evidence of these crises materializing, the cost of student loans and the percentage of students who leave college with debt have increased dramatically in the last few years. From 1995–96 to 2003–04, the percentage of undergraduates who received Stafford loans increased from 25 percent to 33 percent, and the percentage of students who received the far more costly *un*subsidized loans increased from 10 percent to 21 percent (Wei and Berkner 2008, 7). The amount students borrowed increased, too (8). According to the Project on Student Debt, 2009 graduates carried an average of $24,000 in student-loan debt, even as they faced one of the worst job markets in the decade (Project on Student Debt 2010). These figures do not necessarily take into account private loans, such as home-equity loans. The most alarming cases are those students using credit cards to pay for college expenses: a recent study found that undergraduates are carrying record-high credit card balances: 21 percent of undergraduates had balances up to $7000! Ninety-two percent of undergraduates reported charging textbooks and other school supplies, and 30 percent charged tuition (Sallie Mae 2009, 3).

Taking on debt is a risk for all students, whether or not we in the academy are willing to admit it. As Chuck O'Toole puts it, "The notion that not every degree brings more money, and that some education risks may not pay off, is nearly heresy" among those whose job it is to recruit students (O'Toole 2006, 27). Like other kinds of investment, experts recommend that students who take on debt weigh the amount they borrow against their projected income upon graduation, an imprecise science at best. Min-Zhan Lu and Bruce Horner maintain that students' "investment in higher education is materially, intellectually, emotionally, and viscerally costly and risky: it's not clear how, when, or whether the investment will 'pay off,' and what economic, emotional, or intellectual form the 'return' will take" (Lu and Horner 2009, 115). The risks and consequences of student debt have exploded into popular discourse in recent months, in part thanks to the Occupy movement. But in the end, as I discuss above, borrowing for college is almost always a good investment financially, repaid over a lifetime of increased earnings and benefits, better health, and better quality of life.

Assuming, of course, that the student graduates. A student who borrows and then drops out has taken a risk and failed. Like people who borrow a sizable amount to buy a house, only to see the market tank and find themselves under water with a mortgage (how many readers don't personally know someone who has recently been in this situation?), a student who borrows and drops out is left with a product—a semester or two of college—that not only fails to repay the original investment but is actually of lesser value than what is owed. According to one study:

> Nearly one-fourth of borrowers who dropped out . . . had defaulted on at least one loan, most likely resulting in a bad credit rating and other negative consequences for the borrower. . . . Compared with students who borrowed and attained a bachelor's degree, those who borrowed and dropped out were more than twice as likely to be unemployed six years later. If they were employed, they were much more likely to be in low-paying jobs (Gladieux and Perna 2005, 7–8).

This same study found that "more than 20% of borrowers drop out" (Gladieux and Perna 2005, 4). The data for this study came from students who enrolled for the first time in 1995–1996. Since then, the cost of tuition has risen, loans have become more expensive, and subsidized loans have become more difficult to attain, but retention rates have not changed. The numbers quoted here, therefore, are a very conservative estimate of current students who have borrowed sizable amounts of money and proceeded to drop out. A failed investment indeed.

Under these circumstances, leaving college without a degree is not just analogous to failing in business, it is the same thing. And due to the shift in ideology in the nineteenth century, from failure as *a business event* to failure as *an identity*, dropping out is *both . . . and*: it is a serious setback to one's financial future, but it also implicates one's social, and even moral, standing. Sandage quotes Ralph Waldo Emerson, who, writing in his journal, articulated what was a new maxim in the nineteenth century and remains a deep-seated assumption today: "Nobody fails who ought not to fail. There is always a reason, *in the man*, for his good or bad fortune" (qtd. in Sandage 2005, 46). It follows that we are willing to believe it is an individual's fault for dropping out of college: the reason is "in the man." Sandage's history of failure leads him to claim that "failure was intrinsic, not antithetical, to the culture of individualism" (67).

Our complicity in this ideology, our willingness to believe that the reason for failure is indeed, as Emerson suggested, "in the man," enables us as faculty to ignore the terrible financial ramifications for students who drop out for good and those who stop out or transfer to other institutions, losing credits along the way. Moreover, the individualization of failure, I believe, also deflects our attention from more systemic concerns. We are willing to blame the student for leaving, and we may even be willing to blame dumb bad luck, but we have no reason to blame ourselves.

STUDENTS LEAVING COLLEGE: INDIVIDUALS AND INTEGRATION

The individualization of the problem of attrition coincides with the larger ideological context of failure, but it is also perpetuated by the dominant understanding of and approach to the problem of retention. Much of what is considered best practice among retention efforts can trace its lineage to the work of Vincent Tinto. According to Berger and Lyon's history of retention, "Tinto's interactionalist theory of student departure became one of the best known, and most often cited, theories relating to student departure" (Berger and Lyon 2005, 19). The extent to which his work is cited—his 1987 book has been cited 3,467 times, according to Google scholar—is one indication of his influence, as is the extent to which his model has been revised, extended, tested, and reevaluated by other scholars. His work is considered paradigmatic in the field (see, e.g., Braxton and Hirschy 2005, 68; Braxton and Lee 2005, 108). It is a paradigm that still holds tremendous influence, both in the scholarship and in the practices put into place by colleges and universities. In fact, Tinto is the only retention scholar cited in my own institution's 1998–1999 self-study (which I analyze as part of chapter 2). The authors of that document state that "the College drew heavily on the work of Vincent Tinto and other recent research on student success in college. The goals and strategies proceed from the basic assumption in Tinto's work that 'in the interactive reciprocal world of institutional life student retention is at least as much a function of institutional behavior as it is of student behavior'" (Columbia College Chicago 2010a, 219).

Tinto's theoretical model, elaborated most thoroughly in his monograph *Leaving College: Rethinking the Causes and Cures of Student Attrition*, turns on the social and academic integration of individuals into the institutional community (Tinto 1987, 114). According to Tinto, his model corrects for the one-sided perspectives of both the psychological theories and the societal theories that preceded his work (86–89). Retention efforts that arise from this work attempt to "integrate" the individual into the institution in both formal and informal ways. For example, at one institution where I worked, a retention effort required that academic advisors, who were each responsible for a small group of first-year students, not only check in with students regularly and meet with them about their academic progress (intellectual integration), but also plan group activities, such as dinners at a local restaurant or movies on campus (social integration). Likewise, first-year seminars are frequently developed as retention efforts in order to integrate students into the intellectual values of academia, and new, more elaborate orientation programs are contrived to integrate students socially. We see these principles in the recent email from my college president, which I discuss at length in chapter 2: "The college community will place a spotlight on the new undergraduate student experience seeking to better *welcome, integrate, and support* our new students" (italics added).

Due to the sheer number of retention efforts put into place in the past decade, and the prominence of Tinto's model in the discourse of retention, Tinto's influence on the current culture of American college campuses is immeasurable. However, his theory is built entirely on an analogy that limits our understanding of the phenomenon of retention. He draws on Emile Durkheim's study of suicide and argues that of the four forms of suicide Durkheim outlines, it is egotistical suicide that provides an "analogue for our thinking about institutional departure from higher education" (Tinto 1987, 105). Egotistical suicide, according to Durkheim, occurs when individuals fail to integrate socially or intellectually within their communities. While Durkheim was more concerned with the conditions of the *communities* that prevent individuals from successfully integrating, and thus lead to high rates of suicide, Tinto is interested in elaborating a theory that explains why *individuals* leave colleges and universities (105). Therefore, while he maintains Durkheim's focus on social and intellectual integration, he adds to this model an analogue to "suicidal tendency," those personal "dispositions which incline individuals toward departure" (109). It is a student's intentions and commitments—or lack thereof—that determine whether or not the student will successfully integrate into a given college community. Departure from college, according to Tinto, "is taken to reflect the unwillingness and/or inability of the individual to become integrated and therefore establish membership in the communities of the college" (120).

When scholars and retention experts cite Tinto, they rarely question the analogy between suicide and students leaving college, but this analogy should at least give us pause. Though elsewhere in *Leaving College* Tinto states that "if the leaver does not define his/her own behavior as representing a form of failure, neither should the institution," it is worth considering that at the very core of his model lies what many consider the ultimate personal failure: suicide (Tinto 1987, 132). At the very least, this analogy implies that leaving college is bad. Perhaps the willingness of institutions to embrace his model underscores the truth that when students leave a college or university, it is almost always bad for the institution. But leaving is not always bad for the student. The analogy also implies that leaving college is permanent, but neither is this the case for many students who transfer to other institutions or who return later in life. Thus, retention efforts that arise from Tinto's model, based as it is on an analogy to suicide, originate with the assumption that we must prevent something negative from happening. (We hear this in the language of efforts framed as "interventions.") Framed this way, retention efforts are by nature anxious endeavors. Even those efforts not deliberately, or even conceptually, based on Tinto's model that nonetheless aim to *prevent* students from leaving fail to address higher education in positive terms.

Practically and politically, however, the analogy to suicide is more problematic because of the focus on the individual student. Tinto's revision of Durkheim's theory to focus on the "unwillingness and/or inability of the *individual* to become integrated," as opposed to Durkheim's focus on the conditions of the *community* that prevent individuals from integrating, essentially blames the individual for problems much more effectively understood as systemic, institutional problems. Services designed to more successfully integrate individual students— improved tutoring, advising, or counseling services, for example, or living-learning programs, or orientations that partner returning students with small groups of new students—only attempt to align the individual student more thoroughly with preexisting intellectual and social values of the institution. These services do nothing to change the nature of the institution itself. Tinto's discussion of Durkheim's theory alludes to the potential of Durkheim's ideas to drive more drastic institutional reform: Tinto says, "In his concern for social reformation, Durkheim sought to discern the structural attributes of societies which give rise to conditions of malintegration" (Tinto 1987, 103).[1] However, Tinto deliberately diverges from Durkheim in order to develop a "theory of departure that helps explain how various *individuals* come to depart from institutions of higher education" (105; italics added). (And again, while I assert that most retention efforts can trace their roots to Tinto, even among those whose ties to his model are more tenuous, almost all efforts focus on retaining individual students or groups of students who share a single characteristic.)

As I've said elsewhere in this book, some retention efforts are absolutely worthwhile: I could never argue against improved tutoring services, for example. However, *as retention efforts*, projects such as revamping tutoring services are purely reactionary efforts that seek to maintain the current institutional structure at all costs. Students leave institutions of higher education not because they didn't receive adequate attention from faculty, tutors, advisors, counselors, peers, or administrators. Students leave institutions of higher education because the system of higher education in the United States is by nature exclusionary: the value of undergraduate degrees is determined entirely by how few people obtain them. Students must be denied access, either at the point of admission or the point of graduation, in order to sustain the value of a diploma. Thus, people wringing their hands over the problem of students leaving are ignoring or denying the very nature of undergraduate education. Efforts such as improved tutoring aim to integrate individual students more effectively into the intellectual values of the institution, and student-life efforts aim to integrate individual students more effectively into the social values of the institution. None of these efforts, however, change institutional values in ways that will improve access across the board. So while a handful of individual students may persist because of any given effort, we will never see the improved retention rates that administrators, scholars, and politicians claim to want unless the institutional values become radically more inclusive.

In other words, I do not believe we fail as educators when an individual student decides to leave. Our failure is a failure of imagination, our inability or unwillingness to conceive of higher education in terms truly accessible to everyone. The argument I am making here is not new. Scholars of basic writing and disability studies have made this same argument before. Since its roots in open admissions in the early 1970s, basic writing, by virtue of its attention to students from diverse educational, cultural, and socioeconomic backgrounds, has threatened the university's sense of itself. Specifically concerned with issues of access, basic writing puts pressure on the university to reconsider who should be allowed to enter and succeed in higher education. However, throughout the history of basic writing, the impulse to improve access to higher education has been tempered by institutional and material constraints on the (sub)discipline of basic writing itself. One can trace a tension within basic writing, throughout its history, between wanting to claim a legitimate space in the academy in which to do its work on one hand and wanting to radically transform the academy on the other. A single (oftcited) moment in this history illustrates my point.

In 1997, Ira Shor, a leading voice in debates about basic writing and critical pedagogy, published an article in the *Journal of Basic Writing* declaring basic writing to be "our apartheid." He argues in that article that basic writing adds another "layer of linguistic control" to an undemocratic system of tracking and testing in higher education with the effect of slowing basic writing students' progress toward degrees, many times stifling hopes of graduation altogether. The result is that the number of college graduates who would overwhelm an economy that needs cheap labor is contained. His concluding lines are an inspirational rallying cry for an end to basic-writing programs: "Farewell to educational apartheid," he cheers; "farewell to tests, programs and classes supporting inequality; farewell to the triumphant Harvard legacy now everywhere in place, constantly troubled, widely vulnerable, waiting for change" (Shor 1997, 101). In other words, hello to a radically changed university.

The article, as one might expect, generated a heated discussion among advocates of basic writing. Karen Greenberg's response is perhaps the most notable because she shares Shor's affiliation with CUNY and because of their history of contention over the nature of basic writing. Greenberg defends basic writing classrooms as "'safe' contexts" for otherwise marginalized students (Greenberg 1997, 92), and she warns that if "Shor's vision came to pass" and developmental courses were dismantled, then "at least half the students now entering the university where Shor and I teach (CUNY) would be barred [from admission to the university] (94). Shor's vision is not that the students in basic-writing classes would disappear but that they would permeate higher education and in the process change its core values. Greenberg's argument comes from a place of skepticism that such change is possible, and helping individual students succeed in the status quo—providing them "safe contexts"—is perhaps the best we can do.

Disability studies scholar Jay Dolmage provides metaphors that capture the tension we see between Shor and Greenberg. Dolmage argues that universities erect "steep steps" so that "access to the university is a movement upward—only the truly 'fit' survive the climb. The steep steps, physically and figuratively, lead to the Ivory Tower" (Dolmage 2009, 123). Shor, Greenberg, and Dolmage all recognize the fundamentally exclusionary nature of the institution of higher education. For these scholars, then, the question turns on what to do in response to this exclusion. The "retrofit," Dolmage's second metaphor, is the temporary fix, the ramp built for students with physical disabilities, for example, but typically at an out-of-the-way entrance. According to Dolmage, the retrofit is "an after-the-fact construction. It is always *supplemental*—always not originary. The retrofit is additional" (135). To use Dolmage's language, then, basic writing is a retrofit, an after-the-fact add-on meant to get students in the back door. Greenberg's argument is that without this academic ramp, students would never get in the building. Shor's argument is that the ramp does nothing to change the building itself, or the steep-steps mentality at its very foundation. The metaphorical—and sometimes quite literal—back door of the retrofit underscores Shor's claims of apartheid.

My argument here is that retention efforts are a kind of retrofit that, like basic-writing courses or ramps for people with physical disabilities, treat failure as the problem of the individual rather than of the institution. And like basic writing and accommodations for people with disabilities, retention efforts are add-ons typically prompted by external exigencies. Historically, when there have been pressures to increase access to higher education, concerns about retention rates have proliferated. In fact, the first studies of retention—or "student mortality" as it was sometimes called—emerged in the 1930s at a time when enrollments were increasing, as was the value of a college degree, because of the shift to an urban industrialized society and the corresponding need for managers and professionals (Berger and Lyon 2005, 13–14). New demographics of students challenged the willingness and abilities of postsecondary educational institutions to integrate people from diverse backgrounds. Currently, a different kind of external exigency has fueled the retention enterprise: graduation rates are increasingly seen as measures of quality, as key factors in the exercise of accountability, and as the basis for institutional budgets (Hossler 2006; Tinto 2005b, ix).

In other words, in the dominant discourse surrounding retention, the fundamental motivation to improve retention rates is almost always *other* than truly increasing the number of students who have access to a complete, coherent undergraduate education at one college or university. Tinto's model for integrating individual students, and all the retention efforts that have derived from it, foreclose on the possibility of envisioning a radically different institution. Short of that, any retention effort will necessarily fail to yield impressive results if we think of results solely in terms of increased numbers of students who stick around. The problem, as I see it, is the amount of time and money and intellectual energy spent on an impossible project when we could spend all those resources on educating the students in front of us right now.

OPENING UP THE INSTITUTION: EXPANDING KNOWLEDGE, EXPANDING POSSIBILITIES

A radically inclusive institution of higher education would have to revise our traditional narrative of a college education: students and faculty alike tell themselves the story of the protagonist who studies for four consecutive years at a single institution, earning a degree and then a job. In this narrative, the incredible financial investment of four years of college tuition makes sense because the return on the investment is almost certain, and failure is obviously "in the man" who, for whatever reason, doesn't play the role laid out for the protagonist. A different narrative, though, would accommodate plot twists that don't necessarily make sense, conflicts that aren't resolved, characters motivated by unpredictable and sometimes contradictory goals, protagonists who don't complete the story but are not considered tragic.

Part of the failure of the discourse of retention is that it reinforces the traditional narrative of higher education by treating students who leave as individual problems to be solved, situations that require intervention. This discourse does not allow for stories like that of Nathan. In fact, Nathan's story is difficult to tell, not just because it contains a biography's normal twists and turns but because of the moments of tension in his own telling, the contradictory motivations he ascribes to his own actions. His father is an immigrant who came to the United States, and in Nathan's words, *he knows, like, because they didn't have anything there, you came here to become something.* Higher education, for Nathan's father, was a way to "become something," and he attended college on a soccer scholarship. However, when Nathan's older brother was born, his father had to drop out of college to work; he never returned. Nathan's brother attended Northwestern University in Chicago until his junior year but left for a job serving Spanish-language customers at a bank. An average student in high school who enjoyed the support of mentors among his high-school faculty, Nathan himself was counting on a baseball scholarship to college until an injury sabotaged that option. Instead, after high school, he worked (hard) at whatever jobs he could, watching enviously as his friends went off to four-year colleges. He eventually enrolled at one of Chicago's city colleges.

His experience at this two-year college sounds like a case study out of a retention textbook: what not to do. About the initial registration and financial aid service, he says:

> *It was horrible to go through* [the college]*'s financial aid service. You're there nearly, I say, like, four hours because you have to—you go from the ground level to the second floor. From the second floor, you go to the fourth floor. From the fourth floor, you go back down to ground level,*

and then from there, you go all the way up to the seventh floor. By the whole cycle, you've been on nearly every floor . . . and the lines are like, around, like, around the—outside the building, around the block, you know, if you wait until the last minute. But even then, you need all this identification. You need to fill out so many papers. Some of the papers are just repetitive.

About his writing teacher, he said:

It was just, the teacher was—he wasn't there—I don't think he was there full time. And because he worked at [three different colleges and universities in the area]. *But I had trouble with writing. And when I would go—he would only have ten-minute, like, meetings. So, you had to, like, hurry up and say everything that was wrong with your paper or you had trouble with, and after that ten minutes, if you didn't get out everything, then the next one. It was just like a line. It was a line out the door, like, you know, after your ten, you've got to go. There's not two minutes more. That's it.*

About his general impression of college at the time, he said: *I had such a bad experience that it just felt I was like a number.* He only passed two classes and knew early in the semester that he wouldn't be back. After financial aid, he lost $500 to the experience, plus the expense of books. In the context of the discourse of retention, Nathan leaving this college is a failure. On the part of the college, retention experts would target services like financial aid and advising, and admonish faculty to spend more time with students, in order to integrate Nathan more successfully and prevent him from leaving. On Nathan's part, he failed classes, spent money on credits he didn't earn, and left with a very bitter taste for higher education in general.

But the discourse of retention is unable to account for Nathan's ongoing story. At the same time he was enrolled at the city college, Nathan was attending a trade school for construction materials inspectors through a local union. After an apprenticeship, he had a full-time job, and, in his words, *I loved it.* He enjoyed the camaraderie, the collaboration with the architects, engineers, ironworkers, and carpenters. And he was good at it: *As young as I was, I caught on really quick, so a lot of the guys I would work with, they would say, you know, like, you're going to be a great inspector, you know. If the economy doesn't, you know, go bad, you're going to be one of the top inspectors out there.* This was 2008. By September of 2009, Nathan was laid off, and then eventually his contract was terminated because there were too many union members out of work. Construction jobs had simply disappeared, and that industry was among the slowest to recover.

Nathan traveled south for another job, but between the very difficult physical labor and the one hundred-degree temperatures, when the work dried up, he did not regret coming back to Chicago, where he then enrolled at Columbia College. We already see in his story reasons he might give college another try: he saw his high-school friends go off to four-year schools, and his dad's immigrant experience featured higher education as a way to "become something." To the extent that retention scholarship is taking into account transfer students and stop-outs (those who leave for a period of time and return to higher education), we might see his return to college as part of the larger discourse of retention. However, there are real moments of tension in Nathan's own discussion of why he is attending college and what failure and success might mean in the context of higher education; none of the retention scholarship and programs—designed as they are to *prevent* Nathan from leaving—can create a truly accessible institution that accounts for what Nathan brings to it and what he wants out of it.

When asked why he was attending college, he said, *Because I don't want to work hard anymore as far as, like physically, doing the labor intensive jobs.* I asked about his work as an inspector: earlier in our conversation, he only spoke of the very positive features of this job. When explaining why he was enrolled in college, though, he spoke of pushing overflowing wheelbarrows of concrete and laboring outdoors in all kinds of weather. And he sees in his father the consequences of working these types of jobs over the course of a lifetime. He said his dad regrets not finishing college, *because now that he's older, he doesn't kind of want to work anymore. He's kind of tired already because he worked plenty of, like, labor-intensive jobs. And now he's working in construction again, so, yeah . . . and sort of, he's kind of like breaking down a little bit.*

However, avoiding physical labor and the toll it could take on his body isn't enough to explain why Nathan is attending college. He is studying fashion (admittedly an interesting incongruity for the stocky athlete and construction worker), and his career goal is to help create in Chicago the type of fashion scene you might find in New York or LA. He says his objective is *giving back to the city that, you know, helped me out with, you know, building, you know, high-rises and giving me work to do and inspiration.* He sees higher education, and the career he hopes it will provide, as a continuation of his earlier work, a response maybe, to his work in construction, *not* solely a way to escape it.

Moreover, an interesting turn happened when he was describing his motivation to go to college. His father's work history in labor-intensive positions provided both the motivation for getting a college degree and the reasons he might not be able to. He explained:

> *He's getting injured a lot more, because he's still injured. Injured his finger recently. And I see that, and it's like, I know—I tell him, I know you don't want to work, but what else are you going to do, you know? I'm trying to look for a better job, but there's hardly anything out here. I tried to apply here at Columbia, but there's sort of like a waiting list type of thing, and I don't know. It's kind of weird . . . . When my dad got hurt at work, then that's when, you know, we—or, like, as far as living situation, it was just like, you know, there was less and less money. We couldn't, you know, we had to stretch things out more, and it became a lot harder. And I knew, like, what can I, you know—should I stop going to school and find a better job? Should I—I didn't know what to do. And it was affecting me as far as school, like, worrying about if I'm going to come back.*

While Nathan is currently enrolled in school as of this writing, and he is deeply committed to earning his degree, he admits, *If the union would call me back and if I was really hurting, and I couldn't pay for school, I would have to* [leave college and work as an inspector]. *Because I went to school, I got all these certifications . . . so I wouldn't want them to go to waste. And I wouldn't want people who helped me out along the way to think, like, I did this for nothing.* His explanation here suggests that he would leave college because it's too expensive, but it's not just a matter of feeling compelled to leave: he would also be choosing to return to the inspector's job out of a sense of obligation to the education he earned through the union and to the people he worked with.

In light of his own explanation for why he's in school, and why he might leave, for the at-times contradictory obligations he is trying to meet and his changing goals, it is no surprise that his discussion of success and failure is far more nuanced than the discourse of retention allows for. I asked him how he would know if he achieved success, and he replied, *It would be, like, financially, when I don't have to struggle, because I've been struggling for a long time. And I mean, I don't want to seem like it's, oh, it's all about money. But when you're happy, when you feel content, that's like, what I want to feel.* And failure, to Nathan, is "giving up." He continued:

> *I think just throwing in the towel, just saying, you know what, this is too hard for me, and I can't do anymore. I can't shoulder the burden of going to school, not having a good night rest, studying. Just giving up, just throwing in the towel, saying, you know what, it's not for me, and—it's just like, hopefully it never comes to that. But failure's just—yeah, just not continuing, not, you know, just giving up when you have other—I don't know. I just think it's giving up . . . . As far as, like, failure at, like, to go—it's not like I'm dropping out of school to do nothing or to work at a minimum wage job. I'm going back to where I studied, and I got certifications, and I've worked very hard to be a young up-and-coming inspector. So, it's not going from one extreme to the next.*

For Nathan, there is a very important distinction between "giving up" and choosing to return to meaningful work. Nowhere in his discussion of success and failure did earning the degree (or not) come up. Rather, success was about achieving a state of financial security, which he admitted he could achieve through his work as an inspector, and failure is simply giving up; leaving before earning the degree in order to work or because he can't afford tuition is not failure. Nathan owes $13,000 in loans. Is an education worth it? *Yeah, I think so.* Despite the role finances play in his explanation for the reasons he is attending college, he does not describe worth in terms of future income. Instead, he says, *I just believe, like, from my own experiences, I have come across people who really care. . . . Just the ability to expand my own learning and my own knowledge, and be able to express myself like I haven't before, artistically, through essays, and I'm very proud of how—where I've come up until this point.*

By treating all students' leaving as failure, as individual events requiring intervention, the discourse of retention prevents us from envisioning the systemic changes we need to enact in order to create a radically inclusive education that can meet the complicated needs and desires of students like Nathan. In chapter 4, I consider the implications of stories like Nathan's for our teaching in first-year writing and for the institutions we work in.

NOTE

1   According to Tinto, Durkheim even believed that education could be an "alternative mechanism . . . required to restore the health and stability of modern society," but Tinto dismisses this element of Durkheim as "not central to our present concerns" (Tinto 1987, 103).

4

BEYOND RETENTION

My argument throughout this book has been that trying to prevent students from leaving our colleges and universities before they graduate is ineffective at best: an institution can simply do very little, if anything to address the complicated reasons surrounding students' leaving, the fact that students' chances of success are largely determined before they step foot on our campuses, and the reality that a four-year college education earned at one institution right after high school is not typical for the majority of the population anymore. And trying to prevent students from leaving is downright unethical in situations in which staying enrolled does not serve the best interests of the student, or in which the discourse surrounding retention serves only the financial and ideological interests of those in power.

Why, then, study the discourse of retention at all? If retention efforts don't work, what purpose does it serve for those of us who teach first-year writing to pay attention to this discourse as it circulates in our institutions? On one level, I believe it is important simply because retention efforts—reengineered tutoring initiatives, new advising programs, honors courses, first-year seminars, administrative hires—affect every facet of our working conditions as faculty. And retention statistics are more and more frequently used to determine funding for programs, majors, and at the state level, even whole institutions. And for everyone, even those working in institutions that don't experience much attrition, the most compelling reason for faculty to study the discourse of retention is that this discourse puts into relief some fundamental questions about higher education in general and writing instruction in particular. Is a college degree a right or a privilege? What are the responsibilities of institutions of higher education to educate all students who enroll? What role does writing instruction, especially in

DOI: 10.7330/9780874219319.c004

the first year, play in a college education? Is it preparation for future college classes? Preparation for citizenship, work, life beyond college? Or something else altogether? When students leave our institutions before they graduate, we must confront the enormity of these questions. We must consider the value (in all senses of that word) of our pedagogies and curricula for students who leave, whether they leave to transfer to another institution, stop out for a while before returning to earn their degree, or drop out altogether.

In chapter 1, I tell the story of Helen in order to make the point that the idiosyncrasies of an individual's experience make it nearly impossible either to predict the likelihood of whole groups of students leaving an institution or to prevent their leaving. Nathan's story, at the end of chapter 3, extends this point: neither can we anticipate where students will go once they leave our institutions; no one knows how their stories end. Retention scholars in recent years have begun to distinguish between those students who leave for good (referred to as either *dropouts* or *stayouts*), those who leave for a while but return to finish a degree (referred to as *stopouts*), and those who leave an institution in order to transfer to another. All students tend to be counted as lost revenue by the original institution, so up until recently, most institutions have failed to make these distinctions. However, recognizing the different circumstances among students who leave, the retention scholars argue, may enable institutions to target their retention efforts in more subtle ways (see Caison 2004–2005; Mallette and Cabrera 1991; Okun et al. 2008–2009; Wintre et al. 2006). For example, you might target one program at students who have changed their minds about their majors and so intend to transfer to another institution and target another program at students who are struggling academically and so intend to drop out, possibly to return later.

From the perspective of first-year writing administration, curricula, and pedagogy, however, I believe it matters less which students are headed where and more that we can no longer assume a predictable path through higher education for any of our students: retention rates nationally, and at many institutions, remind us that students are transient. They leave. In what follows, I consider the implications of knowing our students will leave and begin to imagine how and what we might teach them while they're still in our classes.

RESITUATING WRITING INSTRUCTION IN THE CONTEXT OF RETENTION

Two recent books, Richard E. Miller's *Writing at the End of the World* and David W. Smit's *The End of Composition Studies*, both use the idea of *the end* heuristically to envision a way forward for writing instruction and English studies and, in the case of Miller's book, for the humanities more generally. In *Writing at the End of the World*, Miller paints a fairly grim picture: Chernobyl, Columbine, 9/11, Operation Desert Storm, the Unabomber. On a personal level, he discusses his father's suicide attempts, and in the last chapter, his father's death. Because the book was published in 2005, evoking the end of the world probably wasn't difficult. I saw Miller speak in the fall of 2009 and he joked that while the main argument of this book is that, in fact, the world was not ending, in 2009 he wasn't so sure. As I write, a year and a half later, Japan has just suffered a devastating earthquake, tsunami, and nuclear crisis, and every other story in the news spells impending doom: the environment, the increasing threat of terrorism, escalating military conflicts, international financial collapse. "Why go on teaching when everything seems to be falling apart?" Miller asks in the preface (R. Miller 2005, x). He continues in chapter 1:

> I have these doubts, you see, doubts silently shared by many who spend their days teaching others the literate arts. Aside from gathering and organizing information, aside from generating critiques and analyses that forever fall on deaf ears, what might the literate arts be said to be good for? How—and in what limited ways—might reading and writing be made to matter in the new world that is evolving before our eyes? Is there any way to justify or explain a life spent working with—and teaching others to work with—texts? (R. Miller 2005, 6)

His answer is that yes, there is a way to justify a life working with texts, mostly because it is in these texts that we can begin to imagine a new world. David Smit's picture is less existentially bleak, but the end—in this case, of the discipline of composition studies—is no less clear. While the title of his book is a play on the word *end*, so his work is also about the purpose, the telos, of writing instruction, Smit takes seriously the possibility that we may have reached the limits of our disciplinary knowledge. In the first half of his book, he argues that as a discipline we have failed to answer some of the basic questions of our field, such as "what is writing?" and "can writing be taught, and if so how?" Moreover, he asserts that "research and scholarship in composition studies have reached a certain limit in their ability to formulate fundamental paradigms, models, and theories about the nature of writing" (Smit 2004, 9). A grim picture for those who are making their careers in either formulating or implementing such paradigms, models, and theories. So where do we go from here?

Both Miller and Smit envision a way forward for writing instruction, and both situate writing instruction in the context of broader curricula in order to do so, in the context of the humanities in Miller's case, and, for Smit, in the context of writing in the disciplines. However, at institutions who may lose up to half their first-year students, the issue of retention forces us to also develop answers in the context of the single semester of writing instruction. Situated as it typically is, at the very beginning of undergraduate curricula, first-year writing may be the one course that practically all college dropouts, stopouts, and transfers across the nation have in common. Due to its place in the curriculum, as Douglas Reichert Powell points out, composition is "one of the most public sites within higher education" (Reichert Powell 2007, 195). This situation presents those of us who teach the course with an astounding amount of responsibility. In my more optimistic moments I think it also presents us with an equally astounding amount of potential. However, unless we think of the course in this way, we won't ever live up to either the responsibility or the potential.

We need to be taking seriously questions like these: What should our courses look like—what should students read and write and do in class—when we know that many of our students won't come back to our institution next year, and that some may never graduate? How might the various approaches to composition, for example digital and multimodal writing, writing in the disciplines, literature-based courses, and so on, fit in a writing curriculum designed for students who may or may not graduate? What is the *value* of my course for those students who never graduate? And for all students, whether or not they graduate? What is my responsibility to those students who leave? The fundamental question of my project expands the relevance of my arguments here to even those institutions that do not see a significant percentage of their students leave: How might we reframe the discourse of retention so it is about educating all of our students, even those who leave, rather than about trying to keep students here?

THE PROBLEM OF TRANSFER IN THE CONTEXT OF RETENTION

As we face our work as writing instructors and program administrators, we must begin with the assumption that students will leave. Some writing instructors at institutions with more generous admissions policies must assume that a significant percentage of the students in their first-year writing classes will leave the institution immediately upon finishing the course. At institutions with the most rigorous admissions policies, instructors can assume that their students will leave their institution with a degree in hand. At all institutions, instructors can assume that some of their students will transfer to other colleges and universities. While we can all assume that our students will leave, none of us can predict where they will go after our class. Will they go on to upper-division classes in other disciplines? Will they go to other institutions? To jobs requiring an advanced degree? To jobs that require very little writing at all? Will they go on to lives steeped in written texts, or not?

Not knowing challenges our sense of purpose, our curricula, and our pedagogies. Asking where our students will go foregrounds the question of transfer—the question of what students take with them when they leave. What can we teach our students about writing that will transfer to the varied contexts they will find themselves in? Like many of the other questions writing professionals must ask themselves, the question of transfer is fundamentally transformed —in productive ways, I believe—when asked in the context of the problem of retention.

Composition studies as a field has begun to ask the question of transfer more earnestly in recent years; in their 2009 article titled "Pedagogical Memory: Writing, Mapping, Translating," Susan C. Jarratt, Katherine Mack, Alexandra Sartor, and Shevaun E. Watson refer to an "explosion of studies about transfer" in which scholars are taking up "the most difficult question for the profession—how and when does writing instruction matter to students in the long run?" (Jarratt et al. 2009, 46). What the problem of retention does is revise our sense of "the long run": while many studies about transfer see that run being a relatively straight route into upper-division disciplinary courses, the problem of retention highlights the fact that the run may be better envisioned as a series of short sprints in a variety of directions, interspersed with long slow rambles and even extended periods on the bench with relatively little writing activity going on in an individual student's life.

Research on transfer in the field of the science of learning indicates that achieving expertise in any given domain, whether it is writing, chess, or physics, requires not just extraordinary amounts of time but also motivation to learn and educational contexts that closely overlap with the contexts in which the expertise is to be applied (see Bransford, Brown, and Cocking 2000, especially chapters 2 and 3). Time (and lots of it), motivation, and analogous contexts for writing are essential: however, none of these is easy to achieve in the first-year classroom, and some may simply be impossible. It is not surprising, then, that in the field of composition studies, research on transfer of writing skills yields disappointing conclusions. In their article, Jarratt, Mack, Sartor, and Watson review the research on transfer in composition studies, citing the most prominent studies—those of Nancy Sommers and Laura Saltz, Anne Herrington and Marcia Curtis, and Lucille McCarthy, among others—and admit that the results are "sobering" (Jarratt et al. 2009, 46). Moreover, Jarratt, Mack, Sartor, and Watson's own study of approximately one hundred student writers in their junior and senior years came to conclusions very similar to this earlier research in the field: even the most successful students in their study "lacked fluency in basic writing terminology, failing to identify genres beyond the most basic ("research paper") or to distinguish modes of development, such as summary and analysis" (48). David Smit frames the issue of transfer in writing instruction more broadly but not at all more optimistically: "We cannot assume that writers will transfer the kinds of knowledge and skills they have learned previously to new writing tasks. Such transfer is unpredictable and depends to a great degree on the student's background and experience, over which the instructor has little control" (Smit 2004, 130).

These grim conclusions about transfer are tempered somewhat by the work of Marilyn Sternglass and, more recently, of Sommers and Saltz. In both of these longitudinal studies, the researchers recognize that, in Sternglass's words, "writing development occur[s] neither neatly nor linearly" (Sternglass 1997, 297). As Sommers and Saltz write, "For all the students in our study, learning to write has been a slow process, infinitely varied, with movements backward and forward, starts and stops, with losses each time a new method or discipline is attempted" (Sommers and Saltz 2004, 145). The benefit of the longitudinal study is that one can recognize both the movements backward *and* the movements forward. What Sternglass contributes to the understanding of students' writing development over time is her attention to the ways the students' lives outside the classroom influence their academic performance. The issue of retention highlights the importance of recognizing the nonacademic factors in a student's educational trajectory, and Sternglass's work is particularly valuable in this context because it connects these extracurricular problems and responsibilities specifically to a student's development of writing skills, something retention research does not do. With this perspective, it is much easier to appreciate the reasons a student might learn writing in fits and starts.

In the context of retention, it is worth reminding ourselves that we do not learn how to write once and for all: the frustration we feel when a student leaves our institution midsemester, or even after our course is over, is alleviated somewhat by the hope that our course is not the last place they will practice writing. What this suggests is that we may simply be asking the wrong questions about transfer altogether: we are asking questions that assume a predictable chronology, that ignore the "movements backward and forward, starts and stops" that Sternglass's students experienced. One major problem is that the research in composition studies on transfer occurs almost entirely in the context of the students' academic writing in subsequent semesters at the same institution. Almost all the research asks what concepts, skills, or habits transfer from first-year writing *to writing in other college courses*. In part, this limitation is due to the logistics associated with studying the writing habits of people who have left the institution. Sternglass, for example, says matter of factly, "In my study, I could, of course, follow only those students who remained at the college and who agreed to continue my study" (Sternglass xiii). However, this limitation is due in part to our own disciplinary history and inclinations. Sommers and Saltz, for example, set out to study only students' experiences with undergraduate writing at their own institution and "the role writing plays in helping students make the transition *to* college" (Sommers and Saltz 2004, 127; italics in original). For Sommers and Saltz, located at Harvard, this approach was appropriate considering that the vast majority of their first-year students (as many as 88 per cent) would graduate from Harvard. However, in the context of the issue of retention at many other institutions, the design of their study limits its applicability to only those students who graduate from the institution in which they took first-year writing.

Elizabeth Wardle, in a 2007 article about transfer and the preliminary results from her own longitudinal study, maintains the field's limited focus on transfer from first-year writing ("first-year composition" in her article) to students' courses across the university. While her arguments about the importance of teaching meta-awareness about writing and language are consistent with studies of transfer in educational psychology and the science of learning, she limits her conclusions to the context of writing in college: "What FYC can do, however, is help student [sic] think about writing *in the university*, the varied conventions of different *disciplines*, and their own writing strategies in light of various *assignments* and expectations" (Wardle 2007, 82; italics added). In another article, which Wardle coauthored with Douglas Downs, they remind readers that there is no such thing as a universal academic discourse that we can teach in FYC and that will transfer to other courses (553); instead, they argue, we should teach FYC as an introduction to writing studies, which teaches the meta-awareness central to achieving transfer. However, the underlying assumptions about and goals for the course remain tethered to the practice of writing in the academy. Downs and Wardle argue that such a course will "help students understand *how writing works in the academy so that they can succeed there*" (Downs and Wardle 2007, 578; italics added). (Unrelated to their goals for student writing, but underscoring their focus on the academy, is their larger goal to institute a curriculum that will "lead us [the field of composition studies] further toward full disciplinarity" [578].)

What the issue of retention reminds us is that success for many of our students may not happen in the academy. The work on transfer in composition studies often concludes by highlighting the need for writing in the disciplines and across the curriculum, or, as in the case of Downs and Wardle, a writing major. In the context of retention, however, the question of transfer puts a renewed emphasis on the first-year course: as I've said elsewhere, first-year writing may be the one course all college dropouts across the nation have in common, whether their long run brings them back to college or not. Therefore, rather than simply envisioning pedagogy and curricula that will transfer to next year's biology or history class, confronting the vagaries of our students' educational lives puts our courses up against their lives as workers, citizens, and family members, and as students navigating the bureaucracies and norms of other academic institutions. Of course, first-year writing has always been about these various contexts, but the question of retention puts a greater focus on the *variety*. While this variety puts a heavier burden on our writing instruction, it may also bring a greater relevance. To ask, as most of the research on transfer in composition studies does, What do our students take with them from our course into their other courses at our institution? completely disregards the experience of those students who do not go on to enroll in other courses, or do not enroll in other courses until months or years later, often at other institutions. However, I am not simply arguing that we need to redesign our research on transfer to include the experience of students who leave. I believe that any meaningful, substantial research on transfer that takes into account all the various contexts in which our students end up could well be logistically, methodologically, even conceptually impossible.

Rather, retention helps us recognize that all of our students experience higher education as a much more porous institution than our research recognizes. Johnathan Mauk argues, in "Location, Location, Location: The 'Real' (E)states of Being, Writing, and Thinking in Composition," that "although the average college student is impossible to profile, a vast number of college students share a common trait: they are unsituated in academic space" (Mauk 2003, 369). His point here is that neither our students, nor we as faculty, can imagine a coherent academic space, with its "attendant postures, behaviors, and perspectives," into which our students enter for an uninterrupted period of time (368). While I agree that this is the case, and an especially salient point in the context of retention, I argue that to refer to students as "unsituated in academic space" denies the possibility that many of our students are fully present in our classrooms and very invested in our instruction during the time they are in front of us. It may be useful to understand Mauk's students' struggles not as a problem (only) of space but also as a problem of time: too much of higher education assumes an uninterrupted chronology. The "constant movement away from campus" Mauk concerns himself with occurs not just in space; those movements interrupt curricula that assume subsequent semesters (369). Rather than try to address the "apparent *placelessness* of many new college students" (370), I think it is important to understand that they may indeed be situated in multiple places, right now and across time, and one of those places is indeed our classroom. The concept of kairos is useful here because it shifts our attention away from chronology and toward the opportunities available in a given moment, in a specific place. Indeed, in the first appearance of the term (in the *Iliad*), *kairos* carried a spatial meaning (Sipiora 2002, 2).

The question of transfer is ultimately a question about the purpose of our pedagogy and curriculum in first-year writing. When we ask this question in terms of what knowledge and skills transfer to these other contexts, we are assuming that the purpose of first-year writing is to prepare students for other contexts, typically assumed to be courses in other disciplines. The issue of retention compels us to reevaluate that assumption: when we confront the reality that many of our students leave, and that their writing lives after, *even during*, first-year writing are completely unpredictable, we confront the impossibility that our course could ever prepare all of them for every writing task they may face. The question of transfer always implies a specific target, a specific context to which the learning is applied. There is simply not a single target we can shoot for; there are multiple targets, and they're all moving in and out of focus. Lu and Horner note that a pedagogy intended to prepare students for future contexts may be both practically and politically problematic:

> We refer here not only to the issue of whether any "general writing skills" might or can "transfer" to the work of writing conducted outside the first-year composition course. That possibility has been under serious challenge for some time now. . . . We

also refer to the sustainability of such a promise. Given the scope
and speed of changes and the degree of instability at all levels of
life in recent years—environmental, geopolitical, social, cultural,
and economic—it's unclear what skills might and might not be
marketable at any given time or place, nor is it certain that those
that were would long remain so. (Lu and Horner 2009, 126)

The frustration we hear in the transfer research—the lamentation over the fact that what we teach doesn't seem to stick
when students are in other courses—would turn to a paralyz-
ing depression if we were somehow able to measure what sticks
(and what doesn't) when they leave school to work retail or stay
home to take care of family, or when they enroll in another
institution.

But rather than wallow in the impossibility of it all, we must
see that the problem of retention completely reframes the
questions we ask. If we can't assume that our course prepares
students for future contexts, either in school or out, we must
instead identify other goals for the course. Retention forces
us to simultaneously take the longer view (beyond the upcoming semesters) *and* focus on now. What most research on transfer tells us anyway is that if we need an accurate picture of an
individual's development as a writer, we must acknowledge the
fits and starts, the movements forward and backward, and this
requires the long view. The issue of retention underscores the
significance of this point because as individuals encounter new
situations—other courses, but, if they leave our institution, also
new schools, jobs, personal situations, social media—they must
acquire new writing habits. When we take the long view, we
maintain a healthy perspective on the role of our course in that
trajectory: we can assume that ours is not the last place students
will ever practice and develop their writing.

BEYOND RETENTION: TOWARD A KAIROTIC PEDAGOGY

In the long view, first-year writing occupies a brief moment in
the student's writing life. When I am mindful of the problem
of retention, when I look out at a new group of students and

recognize that a significant percentage of them will not graduate from my institution, I become mindful of the importance of now. My course is important because it is going on right now and I don't know where my students are headed after this. The issue of retention focuses my pedagogy on what my students are doing right *now*, rather than what they may do when they leave my course.

A pedagogy that confronts the porous nature of higher education is a kairotic pedagogy. We are not preparing them for some future context; we are taking advantage of the moment we are in. I began thinking about this approach during a conference panel I was on at CCCC in 2008; Tom Fox served as the chair of the panel. I presented my rather bleak arguments about retention, and during the discussion period, Fox responded to my pessimism with a phrase that has stuck with me ever since and has informed the evolution of this project in significant ways: *participation, not preparation.* (I have not been able to find this phrase in print, but Fox deserves full credit.) Our goal should not be to *prepare* a student to live the life of an intellectual, worker, and citizen, but rather to invite the student to *participate now* as reader and writer of the world, to recognize that they are currently intellectuals, workers, citizens. This focus on *the now* is an embracing of the concept of kairos, of learning to recognize the opportunities that arise because of a particular conjunction of forces in a given moment rather than the obligations that arise at a particular point in chronological time.

Such an approach does not dictate a specific kind of curriculum but instead encourages a kind of attitude toward course design. Rather than begin with a list of discrete skills we think our students might need in future courses or contexts, skills or habits that may or may not transfer, we begin with writing and reading tasks that are important here and now in the lives of engaged students, workers, citizens. This approach requires a shift in how we frame our course goals and assignments: it is a matter of understanding our goals and assignments in terms of teaching students to seize the opportunities available to them in the context they are currently in and making sure that context—subject matter and intellectual tasks—fosters their immediate engagement. Mauk cautions against the pedagogical cliché of basing a pedagogy on "where students are": "The ultimate objective for a pedagogy that begins where students *are* is to lead students where they are *not*: to academia. The idea, it seems, is to take students from somewhere outside of academia and draw them inward" (Mauk 2003, 374). The issue of retention and a kairotic pedagogy rewrite this cliché: we don't begin where students are in order to lead them toward subsequent semesters in the academy; we begin where students are in order to demonstrate to them the role writing can play in their lives right now, the habits and practices that can, immediately and in the future, infuse their lives as students but also as workers and citizens.

This is not to say our courses must be filled with current events or pop-culture references. What matters, I believe, is that our course goals—the habits and practices we intend to teach— are relevant to real problems and questions that circulate in the students' lives. What types of engagement with texts, what reading and writing and research practices, what habits of mind are most relevant to this group of people in front of me *right now?* Clearly, answers to these questions shift from institution to institution, from semester to semester, and—as our students face the types of situations that might lead them to leave our college or university—even from week to week. John E. Smith states, "Kairos means a time of tension and conflict, a time of crisis implying that the course of events poses a problem that calls for a decision at that time, which is to say that no generalized solution or response supposedly valid at any or every time will suffice" (John E. Smith 2002, 52). No generalized syllabus or assignment is sufficient as a response to the types of crises our students face; a kairotic pedagogy is flexible and inventive enough to determine what reading and writing tasks a student might need right now. Moreover, an instructor who embraces a kairotic pedagogy will see a student's financial or family crisis as more than a problem to be solved: Smith continues, "Kairos means that the problem or crisis has brought with it a time of opportunity . . . for accomplishing some purpose which could not be carried out at some other time" (52). An incident like Helen's car accident, which can derail a student's best efforts, is a problem that requires inventive responses, but, moreover, it's an opportunity to teach a student something about reading and writing you couldn't teach at any other time.

Miller argues that kairos "resists method" (C. Miller 2002, xiii); likewise, Debra Hawhee argues that a kairotic approach to rhetoric (and I would add, to the rhetorical act of teaching) "troubles programmatic approaches" (Hawhee 2002, 32). As such, my argument here seems to work against any attempts I might make to spell out what just such a pedagogy might look like, or to describe in detail what it might mean for a curriculum to be inventive in the face of the radical particulars of our students' lives. Nevertheless, a pedagogy motivated by kairos can take place in a number of types of writing courses—courses developed around a particular theme, discipline-specific writing courses, courses in new media, and more—and the examples I offer below should be relevant to instructors teaching in institutions that experience high rates of attrition as well as those with high retention rates. Before I get to the examples, I am willing to claim that one type of assignment does *not* belong in a course informed by kairos: any assignment that begins with "Pretend you . . ." announces a disconnect between the real rhetorical situations our students face every day and the task at hand; such an assignment is not paying attention to the particulars of the time and place the classroom occupies and what should be substantial ongoing conversations that the course material has given rise to.

These conversations could arise from a variety of course materials, and a kairotic pedagogy might take as its focus any number of themes. For example, studying the theme of *work* makes sense because all students work in school, and many work in paid positions. Thus, scholars and teachers like Tony Scott and Min-Zhan Lu and Bruce Horner are useful resources for designing a kairotic pedagogy. Scott, for example, describes a writing class that focuses on work as an ongoing aspect of students' lives as well as the many issues associated with work in contemporary political economy. . . . Students write about their own lives as workers, they interview others about aspects of the work they do, they examine the discourses of work on the job and at school, and they research broad topics that shape the terms of work in and out of education. (Scott 2005, 162)

What is important here is the focus on students' current work, both in paid jobs and at school, not on skills they may need in possible future careers. Lu and Horner describe a similar approach, in which students study terms such as *career, mobility*, and *marketable skills*, and identify how the meanings of these terms fluctuate in different contexts (school, neighborhood, etc.) and in different economic and geopolitical frameworks (Lu and Horner 2009, 125). Lu and Horner argue that "literacy skills for studying global forces from 'below'—in terms of inclusive distinctions and how they are charged and changed as they travel across differences—are the kind of *life* skills all (job) seeker-consumers do need to survive and thrive" (126; italics in original). Identifying these as *life* skills highlights the value of a course with such a focus, not as preparation for the future but as important in students' lives at all times, including right now.

The courses that Scott and Lu and Horner describe share the common feature of studying *work* as a central theme in students' and faculty's lives, but any theme that invites students to participate in the exploration of issues and questions that matter to them can embrace a kairotic pedagogy. Likewise, courses that investigate current discipline-specific issues can espouse a kairotic approach. The rhetorical approach to writing in the disciplines assumes that disciplinary knowledge is not a static body of content but rather an ongoing, active way of knowing or doing (Carter 2007, 387). The disjunction between WID professionals and the faculty they work with across campus is created by this disjunction between these two understandings of how disciplinary knowledge works—as content versus process (387). The innovative first-year writing program at Duke gets past this unproductive binary and provides a model for a kairotic pedagogy that is situated in the student's first year but that also immerses students in disciplinary knowledge[1]. Taught by postdoctoral fellows from a variety of disciplines, the themes/titles of different sections range from Freudian Legacies to Interpreting Slavery, from Stages of Life to Media Nation (Hillard and Harris 2003, 16). The course is designed not to give the students disciplinary content knowledge nor to provide specific writing or research skills that transfer to their disciplines; rather, the course is designed to work toward

> writing that works to move knowledge forward and that clearly earns its new conclusions. Such writing doesn't merely quote from other texts but, rather, constructs its point from an interested reading of them. In social terms, *such student writing actively joins rather than listens to the conversation of other thinkers.* (Hillard and Harris 2003, 17; italics added)

First-year writing courses like these invite students to participate in conversations going on right now in the disciplines and to create classroom communities that intersect with those conversations in meaningful ways. The classroom neither models the intellectual activity of the disciplines nor prepares students for it. The goal is active, engaged writing that emerges from "interested reading" and a classroom that seizes the opportunity of the particular confluence of forces and personalities in the room right now.

It is worth noting that this example comes from an institution that does not have to worry about retention (Duke currently boasts a 94 percent graduation rate). However, I argue that this is the type of course we should be teaching at institutions that do worry about retention. I think about the students whose stories I've told in this book, whose relationships to specific colleges or universities are quite tenuous. A course that aims to give them skills or disciplinary content they are supposed to build on in later semesters will be less valuable to them if they leave than a course that involves them in meaningful intellectual tasks, immerses them in written texts and face-to-face conversations, and provides them the opportunity to participate in ongoing significant issues. Even, and especially, a basic-writing course, populated by students most at risk for leaving, should teach students how to approach the intellectual tasks of reading, writing, and talking about complicated problems *in the very same moment* they are engaging in these tasks.

Right now, for everyone, the intellectual tasks themselves—of reading, writing, and conversing about ideas—are in tremendous flux. The modes and media available in a wired world are challenging and changing how we produce and engage with texts and with other people. It is too early (at least for me) to know precisely how this intellectual work is changing, but it is clear we are entering, or are probably already in, an historical period that demands kairotic pedagogies more than ever. While it is beyond the scope of this project to discuss the countless implications of new media and multimodality for writing instruction, I do want to point to the usefulness of kairos for our field as we begin to confront those implications.

Gunther Kress notes that "the participatory affordances of current media technologies blur former distinctions of production and consumption, of writing and reading" (Kress 2010, 144).The ways in which the Internet enables writers to engage immediately with their readers is perhaps the most fundamental change our field must confront. Readers are able to respond immediately to the texts they are reading; multiple authors can produce texts together (the obvious example is in wikis) in ways that put an individual's acts of writing and reading right next to each other and next to other individuals' acts; authors are able to embed other authors' texts into their own in ways that go far beyond traditional acts of citation; and individuals can contribute to and draw on the infinite stores of data available in the forms of written texts, images, music, video, and many other modes. Kress refers to these as "*participatory* affordances"; *participation* is arguably the most important verb in the online world. Participation, not preparation. Our pedagogies cannot prepare students for this world, in part because it is changing so fast it is not realistic that we could anticipate what our students would need a year from now. But more importantly, one cannot "practice" new media technologies without *already* participating.

Kairotic pedagogies, therefore, are ideally suited to the demands of new media and multimodal composition. Hawhee suggests that "kairos thus might be read to mark the celerity and multi-directionality of discourse" (Hawhee 2002, 21). What is more fast moving and multidirectional than the Internet? But kairos doesn't just describe the demands of this changing world; it provides a framework for participating in it. Miller explains a kairotic approach this way: "The challenge is to invent, within a set of unfolding and unprecedented circumstances, an action (rhetorical or otherwise) that will be understood as uniquely meaningful within those circumstances" (C. Miller 2002, xiii). Up until this point, I have been describing pedagogical action that might be meaningful in a classroom that presents "unfolding and unprecedented circumstances," such as students leaving or facing crises that interrupt their education. Kairos should inform what teachers do, I argue.

However, I have also found it increasingly useful to introduce the concept of kairos to my students as well, to weave into my courses readings about kairos and ask them to apply the term to their reading and writing in the course. This works well for emerging texts; students might, for example, study and participate in comment threads on trending articles online. But it works equally well for more slow-moving conversations, like those that happen in scholarly articles; for example, it is important in a course like the ones offered at Duke, which focus on a discipline-specific problem, to help students recognize the rhetorical moves authors make to create the opportunity for them to participate in the ongoing debate. (This approach is the basis for the popular textbook *They Say, I Say* by Gerald Graff and Cathy Birkenstein [2009].) It is a matter of teaching students how to seize the moment in a rhetorical situation, to "invent an action . . . that will be understood as uniquely meaningful" in a particular set of circumstances (C. Miller 2002, xiii).

In terms of the problem of retention, the purpose of a kairotic pedagogy like the ones I describe, or of introducing the term *kairos* to our students, is to recognize the reality that students will leave, some with a degree, others without. Mauk calls for courses that enable students to "conceive the space outside of the campus, outside of the classroom, as academic. And the academic space needs to be conceived as transportable and mutable—as something that is tied to being, rather than to exclusive material surroundings" (Mauk 2003, 380). Mauk is arguing for creating access to higher education for students who are alienated by the physical and conceptual space of campus, for whom "academic space is not an integral part of their intellectual geography" (369).

This kind of opening up of academic space is important, but for students who leave before graduating, the physical place of the college campus could potentially act as a centripetal force, a place to which they can return again and again. So I would extend Mauk's argument to include an opening up of our sense of time as well, to include kairos as well as chronos. For students like Helen, Cesar, and Nathan, higher education does not occur in a tidy chronological package of four years: college serves the needs of these students in different ways at different times. In fact, they come to us as different people at different times: Nathan, for example, was a totally different student in my classroom than he was in the city college classroom two years earlier. Students leaving is not a problem to solve, and it certainly isn't a problem individual faculty can solve in their classrooms. Rather, kairos refocuses our inventive energies on realizing the potential in each group of students, each semester.

BEYOND RETENTION: INSTITUTIONAL CHANGE

I'd like to return to the work of Jay Dolmage, whom I discussed in chapter 3. In that chapter, I used his metaphors of the steep steps and the retrofit to describe, respectively, the exclusionary nature of higher education and the after-the-fact nature of retention programs that try to keep students enrolled. Dolmage offers the principle of universal design as an alternative to the steep steps and retrofit. Initially, and primarily, concerned with students with disabilities, universal design refers to the intentional design of a physical environment that, among other things, is "useful and marketable to people with diverse abilities"; that is flexible, simple, and intuitive to use; that "communicates necessary information effectively to the user"; and that "minimizes hazards and the adverse consequences of accidental or unintentional actions" (Dolmage 2009, 135). But Dolmage argues that these same principles can be used to guide composition pedagogy and curricula and indeed whole institutional cultures. The verb *design* is intentionally active and calls on us to assume responsibility for shaping the institutions we are a part of. As we do the work of designing institutions truly accessible to everyone, Dolmage argues, we are compelled to "see spaces as multiple and in-process . . . UD, then, responds to compression and decay not with panic, but with planning. UD is *kairotic*, in this sense, seeking the opportune, but also acknowledging that context forever shifts" (136). The idea of universality, while troubling to some, as Dolmage points out, at the same time reminds us that "disability is something that is *always* a part of our worldview" (135).

Universal design, as a metaphor and a set of principles, is useful in the context of retention because it allows us to imagine a way forward. Because it is intentionally active and assumes responsibility on the part of those who embrace the concept, faculty must recognize their role in the issue of retention. The discourse of retention as it currently circulates in our institutions is very effective at denying faculty agency in a couple of different ways. First, too often retention efforts are imposed top down by administrators, in both the academic and student-life arms of the institution, who have been assigned to raise retention rates. Faculty are seduced into participating in these initiatives with the promise that it will help the students; when seduction doesn't work, the threat of reduced resources will. The second way faculty are denied agency is through a careful reading of the research itself: most data suggest there is little we can do to prevent students from leaving, although certain characteristics—for example, high-school GPA, parents' level of education, test scores—can accurately forecast that a student is going to leave college without a degree. To a large extent, this data has driven my arguments in this book: I grew increasingly skeptical about all the efforts initiated at my institution, and the amount of money and time they took away from more promising educational efforts, when I knew there wasn't much we could do. However, this data assumes the current structure of higher education. What the concept of universal design does is compel us to envision and design new structures, not simply retrofit old ones, that open up higher education to everyone. We begin to understand our responsibility for devising courses and curricula, but perhaps also admissions and advising models, that assume from the very beginning that higher education should serve everyone who enrolls at various times and places.

Moreover, just as universal design compels us to "see spaces as multiple and in-process," in the context of retention we might begin to see not just space in this way but also curricula and writing instruction as "multiple and in-process." The first-year course becomes an important focal point perhaps for a student's experience with producing, consuming, and circulating texts. But rather than imagine a direct path from this course into courses in other disciplines, for example, or even into certain careers, we begin to understand our course as opening up onto any number of other experiences with writing. Precisely what this implies for our curricula or pedagogy must be determined by taking advantage of the students, the places, the circumstances in front of us. We can do this reenvisioning intentionally—we must take seriously the *design* part of UD—and we can do this reenvisioning freed from the burden of transfer and service to other disciplines.

When Dolmage insists that "disability is something that is *always* a part of our worldview" (Dolmage 2009, 135), it is not to suggest that everyone is disabled, although we all share "the experience of the limitations of the body" (Davis qtd. in Dolmage 136). Rather, universality in this case means that "one of the central tenets of UD is that it helps all students regardless of disability" (135). This concept supports the core argument of my book: to turn the discourse of retention into a call to educate all the students in front of us rather than simply trying to get them to stay. Dolmage argues that universal design is "not a tailoring of the environment to marginal groups; it is a form of hope, a manner of trying" (136). Universal design compels us to design an institution that educates all students, those who may not graduate from our institution in four years right alongside those who will.

BEYOND RETENTION: AND BACK AGAIN

Part of the difficulty of imagining a pedagogy, curriculum, and institution that serves *all* of our students, even those who leave before they earn a degree, is that our understanding of higher education is circumscribed by the idealized version of a two- or four-year stint in one college or university. The discourse of retention reinforces the idealized version of an uninterrupted undergraduate degree because it treats students who leave as a problem to be solved, as a failure to be prevented. The issue of retention in research and in practice tends to have an inflexible perimeter bounded by when a student enrolls in college on the one end and by when a student graduates or leaves on the other. The stories of Helen, Cesar, and Nathan do not have such clear boundaries; they are unfinished, perpetually written and rewritten. There is not even a college chapter in their stories, with a beginning and end; college is a thread that runs throughout. If the discourse of retention is to serve any purpose for us it will be to compel us to imagine how our institutions and classrooms might transform and expand to account for our students' ongoing stories.

For this reason, I now return to the stories of Helen, Cesar, and Nathan. As I noted in the introduction, I do not intend for these stories to be evidence for any of my arguments, nor representative of students in general. Rather, paradoxically, the unique trajectory of each of their stories reminds us how little we know about, and how little we can control, our students' educational careers. Not only is there very little we could have done to prevent them from leaving, the stories of what happened after these students left college testify to the impossibility of designing a curriculum or pedagogy that prepares students for what lies ahead.

Nathan didn't really leave his first college; he simply didn't return after an unsuccessful and unsatisfying semester. In chapter 3, I tell the story of what happened to Nathan after he left his first college—first an apprenticeship, then a rewarding job as an inspector, then a layoff and frustration, and finally enrollment at the institution where I teach. After three very strong semesters at his current college, despite a brief threat that he would have to leave for financial reasons, at the time of writing this chapter he is currently registered for the upcoming semester.

Cesar explains that he did have to leave college after two semesters for financial reasons: *It had to do something with my father losing his job. You know, for me, I always said money was never going to be an issue, but this time we really, really had a bad situation in it.* Cesar had just quit his own job toward the end of the summer between his first year and what was supposed to be his second year in order to focus on school when his father was laid off from his construction job. The family simply couldn't afford tuition. While his mother and sisters were upset that Cesar had to leave college, his father *didn't care;* according to Cesar, *It was like, oh, another thing off his back, off his hands . . . he didn't have to work to put me in school anymore.* Cesar says that not returning to classes was very difficult; he didn't want to do anything, didn't go out for almost a month. *I kind of lost myself.* Then through contacts he had made while in college, Cesar found a job in the music business, his major while he was enrolled, working for a local independent record label on event planning and scheduling tours. He now works at a club where he does a little of everything, from dealing with the bands to working the ticket counter to updating the Facebook page. He lives with his family, as he did when he was enrolled in college.

In chapter 1, Helen describes a car accident that made transportation to school nearly impossible, the loss of the laptop that had promised to make doing homework much more efficient, a change of heart about her major, and a very unstable living situation. Any one of these could have provided the reason she left after one semester. Two years later, though, when asked for the reason she left college, while she did say *I had to get out of my house*, her first response was this: *I left college because I had a hunger for money.* In my mind, this is less a reason for her leaving college and more a rationale for what happened next: she got a job selling for AT&T, door to door, and then was promoted into what she describes as team management, making $1,500 to $2,000 a week. She rented an apartment on her own, bought a car, adopted a dog. But then she lost the job and had to take work at Family Dollar, couldn't make rent, couldn't afford car insurance, couldn't afford food without public aid.

And then she really experienced a setback. *When I left college, I got what I wanted. I got a taste of what is out there. And I realized, like, this is not worth it. I'm wasting my brain, I've got talent, and now I'm working minimum wage jobs.* Eventually, she had to move out of her own apartment, and after a couple of moves, she ended up with a friend selling drugs from a house where *we could only stay in one half of it because the front part had no ceilings . . . we used the oven for heat.* Her friend's arrest provided a reality check. Helen realized that if she, too, was arrested, she would be tried as an adult. The whole scene became a lot more stressful than when she was selling as a kid. She continued to sell for a few more months but also started going back to church and got into Bible study. A different friend—a one-time partier, now on the dean's list in a four-year university—talked to Helen about going back to college. Helen admitted she was scared to go back to college. *And* [the friend] *said, everybody's scared. I'm scared every day, you know.* Helen moved in with her grandmother, and currently she is registered for classes this coming semester at the same city college where Nathan was enrolled his first time through. She chose this college, in part, because of location: it is downtown near where she first went to college (where I teach), her comfort zone. She admits she doesn't know anyone, and she's still scared.

What strikes me about Helen's story, and this is the case for Nathan and Cesar, too, is that college is not really a goal or a destination; these figures imply some degree of finality. Rather, it is one option made available to them at various times in their lives. For Nathan, it became the best option when work in the construction industry dried up, but as he discusses in chapter 3, he still holds open the possibility of returning to his union job as an inspector if that becomes an option again. Likewise, for Cesar, the degree matters—*I definitely want to be still the first to get a degree in college in my family*—but he elaborates: *I do definitely want to go back to school . . . I'm not seeing myself as a failure if I don't go to school, but I still want to go to school. I miss the whole school stuff, interacting with people, finding different people, knowing different people, you know.* Right now, though, he's looking for another part-time job, and college remains a possibility for later on. His long-term goal is still success in the music business, and he says *some people I know don't have a college degree . . . they just go to school to learn how to run a business, and that's what I'm basically learning right now.*

About the period between finishing high school and her return to college this coming semester, Helen remarks: *I've been having a fun, stressful, but blessed journey. Through these past three, four years, I've learned a lot. I've seen a lot. Learned enough. And I'm ready to get back to school.* Returning to college is not the end of that journey, though. Her first semester in college, even though it did not lead to subsequent semesters immediately, opened up that option for later, an option that, compared to selling drugs, now seems worth pursuing. At one point, the military was such an option, but now, she explains, [college] *was a major step, and it was something that I needed because God knows, if I didn't have a taste of what college was like, I might still be on the streets because I wouldn't know where to go back to now.*

Imagine if our institutions were places students could "go back to." Not places where we do everything we can to prevent them from leaving, but places we invite them back to when they're ready. I think again of universal design, which compels us to "see spaces as multiple and in-process . . . UD is *kairotic*, in this sense, seeking the opportune, but also acknowledging that context forever shifts" (Dolmage 2009, 136). For these students, the context of their engagement with higher education shifts over time and space. As students seek "the opportune"—those times in their lives when college is again a possibility, and those places where they might pursue it—what if institutions could respond in kind? Dolmage insists that this view is "not a tailoring of the environment to marginal groups; it is a form of hope, a manner of trying" (136).

Our own courses, too, might seek the opportune. As carefully as we might sequence the courses and the skills we teach, what these students' stories tell me, more than anything, is that each assignment I write, each student paper I read, each semester I teach, must be challenging, rewarding, and substantially educational in itself. Those students who are most at risk for leaving after a semester or two—the underprepared, the basic writers, those pulled away for any of the myriad reasons students leave—are the *least* served by the kinds of pedagogies that isolate narrow skills (skills such as punctuating phrases or practicing subject-verb agreement), even though these populations of students are *most* likely to encounter such pedagogies. This approach to writing instruction assumes students will be able to apply and build on these skills in the *next* course the *next* semester, but for many of these students, *next* is a relative term.

Moreover, not surprisingly, these are not the skills that Nathan, Cesar, and Helen drew on when they left college. In his inspector job after his first semester in college, Nathan had to fill out reports, which he learned how to do from his cousin. Cesar explains that he only writes Facebook status updates for the club where he currently works. Helen claims she did no writing in her sales job. *Been doing a lot of math, adding. I've been working with numbers.*[2]

While the writing they do on the job is quite limited, these three students are remarkably prolific, ambitious, and serious about their writing. When asked what role writing plays in his life, Nathan replied without hesitation:

> *I kind of wanted to write a book. I feel like some of the stories that my family on Mom's side, they tell, I think it's really interesting and I would like to—I feel like my writing's getting stronger and stronger where my confidence is gaining because of that. And I would want to write some*

of that stuff down. A lot of them are already older, so, you know, some of
these stories are not going to be around for a while. But I had an idea of
writing it down.

Where Nathan's book is still in the conceptual phase, Cesar has
actually begun a couple of book projects. *Writing has been always*
a part of my life, he says. One project is about dynamics in families in which the children are not treated well. Another one is
about his own life, his past. And he's always writing music and
poems. For a while there, he said, he was writing every day.

And Helen, too, sees herself as a writer and writes every day.
She keeps a journal with three sections in it: the first section is
for her to-do lists, the second section is for her Bible study, and
the last is for her poems and music. She describes writing as *very*
important. Highly important. . . . That's my venting. . . . I can read
the scripture, and it will probably mean something. But when I write
it, I can remember it, and it sticks out more . . . writing keeps me orga-
nized. . . . If I miss a day of writing, I would be lost.

None of this implies a particular type of pedagogy or curriculum. On the contrary, to me it implies the difficulty of asking
questions about transfer, of trying to design a course that prepares students for the writing they will do in the future. When I
asked Helen and Cesar what they remembered from my course
two years later, they both described very positive memories.
Cesar remembers *the projects. They made me grow up and get to know*
the real world now. (I describe Cesar's projects in chapter 2, and
as I say there, Cesar's projects far exceeded the work required
by my assignments.) Helen remembers very enthusiastically her
classmates and *the feel you had when you're walking into class. It was*
time for business, and she can provide details two years later from
a short story we read and the in-class discussion and writing she
did in response to that story. However, when I asked them what
they learned about writing that they still use, neither could provide specifics. *Not like your talents went to waste or nothing,* Helen
assured me.

And I believe her. To the extent that college is a place that
Helen can *go back to now,* and that writing is a rich part of these
students' lives, I don't think my talents went to waste. Moreover,

what their stories suggest to me is not the failed application of my writing instruction but rather the incredibly impressive talents, experiences, and personalities I can take advantage of in my classroom at any given time. I began the project anxious about students who left. While doing the research, specifically through the Student Faculty Partnership with Success program I describe in the introduction, I did everything possible both in the classroom and out to prevent Helen and Cesar from leaving. And then I watched them leave. In the discourse of retention, their leaving is the end of the story. But truly listening to students' stories, recognizing that these stories continue, we can get beyond retention—and back again to providing an excellent education for all of our students, including those who leave.

NOTES

1. In the interest of full disclosure, I taught in this program in 2000–2003.
2. While my main concern here is writing instruction, I think the issue of retention has just as much to say about the math curriculum. If there was one course I wish all my students had to take, it would be a math course that teaches them how to calculate interest on the loans that they've taken out to pay for college.

REFERENCES

Astin, Alexander W. 2005–2006. "Making Sense Out of Degree Completion Rates." *Journal of College Student Retention* 7 (1–2): 5–17. http://dx.doi.org /10.2190/7PV9-KHR7-C2F6-UPK5.

Astin, Alexander W., and Leticia Oseguera. 2005. "Pre-College and Institutional Influences on Degree Attainment." In *College Student Retention: Formula for Student Success*, edited by Alan Seidman, 245–76. Westport, CT: Praeger.

Baum, Sandy, and Jennifer Ma. 2007. *Education Pays: The Benefits of Higher Education for Individuals and Society.* Washington, DC: College Board. *College Board.* Accessed 27 May 2009. www.collegeboard.com/prod_downloads/ about/news_info/trends/ed_pays_2007.pdf.

Bean, John. 2005. "Nine Themes of College Student Retention." In *College Student Retention: Formula for Student Success*, edited by Alan Seidman, 215–43. Westport, CT: Praeger.

Berger, Joseph B., and Susan C. Lyon. 2005. "Past to Present: A Historical Look at Retention." In *College Student Retention: Formula for Student Success*, edited by Alan Seidman, 1–29. Westport, CT: Praeger.

Berlin, James A. 1987. *Rhetoric and Reality: Writing Instruction in American Colleges, 1900–1985.* Carbondale: Southern Illinois University Press.

Bok, Derek. 2003. *Universities in the Marketplace: The Commercialization of Higher Education.* Princeton, NJ: Princeton University Press.

Bousquet, Marc. 2008. *How the University Works: Higher Education and the Low-Wage Nation.* New York: New York University Press.

Bransford, John D., Ann L. Brown, and Rodney R. Cocking, eds. 2000. *How People Learn: Brain, Mind, Experience, and School.* Washington, DC: National Academy Press.

Braxton, John, Ellen M. Brier, and Stephanie Lee Steele. 2007–2008. "Shaping Retention from Research to Practice." *Journal of College Student Retention* 9 (3): 377–99. http://dx.doi.org/10.2190/CS.9.3.g.

Braxton, John M., and Amy S. Hirschy. 2005. "Theoretical Developments in the Study of College Student Departure." In *College Student Retention: Formula for Student Success*, edited by Alan Seidman, 61–87. Westport, CT: Praeger.

Braxton, John M., and Stephanie D. Lee. 2005. "Toward Reliable Knowledge about College Student Departure." In *College Student Retention: Formula for Student Success*, edited by Alan Seidman, 107–27. Westport, CT: Praeger.

Burke, Kenneth. 1969. "Appendix D: The Four Master Tropes." In *A Grammar of Motives*, 503–17. Berkeley: University of California Press.

Cabrera, Alberto F., Kurt R. Burkum, and Steven M. La Nasa. 2005. "Pathways to a Four-Year Degree: Determinants of Transfer and Degree Completion." In *College Student Retention: Formula for Student Success*, edited by Alan Seidman, 155–214. Westport, CT: Praeger.

Caison, Amy L., ED.D. 2004–2005. "Determinants of Systemic Retention: Implications for Improving Retention Practice in Higher Education." *Journal of*

DOI: 10.7330/9780874219319.c005

College Student Retention 6 (4): 425–41. http://dx.doi.org/10.2190/FBNU -G3CU-JBXR-MVH6.

Carter, Michael. 2007. "Ways of Knowing, Doing, and Writing in the Disciplines." *College Composition and Communication* 58 (3): 385–418. www.ncte.org.

Chaput, Catherine. 2008. *Inside the Teaching Machine: Rhetoric and the Globalization of the U.S. Public Research University.* Tuscaloosa: University of Alabama Press.

College Board. 2011. "The College Completion Agenda." Accessed 22 July 2011. http://completionagenda.collegeboard.org/.

Columbia College Chicago. 2010a. "1998/1999 Columbia College Self Study Report: Volume One." Accessed 2 August 2010. http://www.colum.edu/oie /institutional-research-reports/Self_Study/PDF_Folder/98-99_Self-Study _Volume_One.pdf.

Columbia College Chicago. 2010b. "HLC/NCA Self-Study Report Spring 2009." Accessed 2 August 2010. http://www.colum.edu/oie/institutional-research-reports/Self_Study/PDF_Folder/Columbia_College_Chicago_Self-Study_ Report.pdf.

Columbia College Chicago. 2013. "Fact Book 2012." Accessed 25 February 2013. http://www.colum.edu/Research_Evaluation_Planning/Historic_ Fact_Books/.

Columbia College Chicago. N.d. "Academics." Accessed 2 August 2010. www. colum.edu/Academics/.

Complete College America. 2011. Accessed 22 July 2011. http://www.com pletecollege.org.

Crowley, Sharon. 1995. "Composition's Ethic of Service, the Universal Requirement, and the Discourse of Student Need." *JAC* 15 (2). www.jacweb.org.

Cutrona, C. E., V. Cole, N. Colangelo, S. G. Assouline, and D. W. Russell. 1994. "Perceived Parental Social Support and Academic Achievement: An Attachment Theory Perspective." *Journal of Personality and Social Psychology* 66 (2): 369–78. http://dx.doi.org/10.1037/0022-3514.66.2.369.

Dolmage, Jay. 2009. "Mapping Composition: Inviting Disability in the Front Door." In *Composing Other Spaces*, edited by Douglas Reichert Powell and John Paul Tassoni, 121–44. Cresskill, NJ: Hampton.

Downs, Douglas, and Elizabeth Wardle. 2007. "Teaching about Writing, Righting Misconceptions: (Re)envisioning 'First-Year Composition' as 'Introduction to Writing Studies.'" *College Composition and Communication* 58 (4): 552–84. *JStor*. http://www.jstor.org.emils.lib.colum.edu/stable/20456966.

Fairclough, Norman. 1992. *Discourse and Social Change.* Cambridge, MA: Polity.

Fairclough, Norman. 1995. *Critical Discourse Analysis: The Critical Study of Language.* New York: Longman.

Fairclough, Norman. 2000. *New Labour, New Language?* New York: Routledge.

Fairclough, Norman, and Ruth Wodak. 1997. "Critical Discourse Analysis." In *Discourse as Social Interaction*, edited by Teun van Dijk, 258–84. London: Sage.

Feyaerts, Kurt, and Geert Brone. 2005. "Expressivity and Metonymic Inferencing: Stylistic Variation in Nonliterary Language Use." *Style* 39 (1): 12–36. *Academic Search Complete.*

Fox, Tom. 1999. *Defending Access: A Critique of Standards in Higher Education.* Portsmouth, NH: Boynton/Cook . http://dx.doi.org/10.2307/358972.

Frost, Robert. 2007. *The Collected Prose of Robert Frost.* Edited by Mark Richardson. Cambridge, MA: Belknap Press of Harvard University Press.

Fulkerson, Richard. 2005. "Composition at the Turn of the Twenty-First Century." *College Composition and Communication* 56 (4): 654–87.

Gladieux, Lawrence, and Laura Perna. 2005. "Borrowers Who Drop Out: A Neglected Aspect of the College Student Loan Trend." The National Center for Public Policy and Higher Education. Accessed 10 January 2008. www.highereducation.org/reports/borrowing/borrowers.pdf.

Gladwell, Malcolm. 2008. *Outliers: The Story of Success.* New York: Little, Brown and Co.

Graff, Gerald, and Cathy Birkenstein. 2009. *They Say, I Say: The Moves That Matter in Academic Writing.* New York: Norton.

Greenberg, Karen L. 1997. "A Response to Ira Shor's 'Our Apartheid: Writing Instruction and Inequality.'" *Journal of Basic Writing* 16 (2): 90–100.

Hagedorn, Linda Serra. 2005. "How to Define Retention: A New Look at an Old Problem." In *College Student Retention: Formula for Student Success,* edited by Alan Seidman, 89–105. Westport, CT: Praeger.

Hawhee, Debra. 2002. "Kairotic Encounters." In *Perspectives on Rhetorical Invention,* edited by Janet M. Atwill and Janice M. Lauer, 16–35. Knoxville: University of Tennessee Press.

Hickman, Gregory P., and Garnet L. Crossland. 2004–2005. "The Predictive Nature of Humor, Authoritative Parenting Style, and Academic Achievement on Indices of Initial Adjustment and Commitment to College Among College Freshmen." *Journal of College Student Retention* 6 (2): 225–45. http://dx.doi.org/10.2190/UQ1B-0UBD-4AXC-U7WU.

Hillard, Van, and Joseph Harris. 2003. "Making Writing Visible at Duke University." *Peer Review* 6 (1): 15–17. www.aacu.org.

Horner, Bruce, and Min-Zhan Lu. 1999. *Representing the "Other": Basic Writers and the Teaching of Writing.* Urbana, IL: National Council of Teachers of English.

Hossler, Don. 2006. "Managing Student Retention: Is the Glass Half Full, Half Empty, or Simply Empty?" *College and University* 81 (2): 11–14. *ProQuest Education Journals.*

Integrated Postsecondary Education Data System (IPEDS). 2013. Accessed 25 February 2013. http://nces.ed.gov/ipeds/datacenter/.

Isaacson, Walter. 2007. *Einstein: His Life and Universe.* New York: Simon & Schuster.

Ishler, Jennifer L. Crissman, and M. Lee Upcraft. 2005. "The Keys to First-Year Student Persistence." In *Challenging and Supporting the First-Year Student: A Handbook for Improving the First Year of College,* edited by M. Lee Upcraft, John M. Gardener, and Betsy O. Barefoot, 24–46. San Francisco: Jossey-Bass, a Wiley Imprint.

Jarratt, Susan C., Katherine Mack, Alexandra Sartor, and Shevaun E. Watson. 2009. "Pedagogical Memory: Writing, Mapping, Translating." *WPA: Writing Program Administration* 33 (1–2): 46–73. *Expanded Academic ASAP.* wpa-council.org/archives/33n1-2/33n1-2jarratt.pdf.

Kress, Gunther. 2010. *Multimodality: A Social Semiotic Approach to Contemporary Communication.* New York: Routledge.

Kuh, George D. 2005. "Student Engagement in the First Year of College." In *Challenging and Supporting the First-Year Student: A Handbook for Improving the First Year of College*, edited by M. Lee Upcraft, John M. Gardener, and Betsy O. Barefoot, 86–107. San Francisco: Jossey-Bass, a Wiley Imprint.

Levitz, Randi S., Lee Noel, and Beth J. Richter. 1999. "Strategic Moves for Retention Success." In *Promising Practices in Recruitment, Remediation, and Retention*, edited by Gerald H. Gaither, 31–49. San Francisco: Jossey-Bass.

Lu, Min-Zhan, and Bruce Horner. 2009. "Composing in a Global-Local Context: Careers, Mobility, Skills." *College English* 72 (2): 113–33.

Lundquist, Cara, Rebecca J. Spalding, and R. Eric Landrum. 2002–2003. "College Student's [*sic*] Thoughts about Leaving the University: The Impact of Faculty Attitudes and Behaviors." *Journal of College Student Retention* 4 (2): 123–33. http://dx.doi.org/10.2190/FLAL-7AM5-Q6K3-L40P.

Mallette, Bruce I., and Alberto F. Cabrera. 1991. "Determinants of Withdrawal Behavior: An Exploratory Study." *Research in Higher Education* 32 (2): 179–94. http://dx.doi.org/10.1007/BF00974436.

Mauk, Johnathon. 2003. "Location, Location, Location: The 'Real' (E)states of Being, Writing, and Thinking in Composition." *College English* 65 (4): 368–88. http://dx.doi.org/10.2307/3594240.

Mautner, Gerlinde. 2005. "The Entrepreneurial University: A Discursive Profile of a Higher Education Buzzword." *Critical Discourse Studies* 2 (2): 95–120. http://dx.doi.org/10.1080/17405900500283540.

Mayr, Andrea. 2008. *Language and Power: An Introduction to Institutional Discourse*. New York: Continuum International.

McNenny, Gerri, ed. 2001. *Mainstreaming Basic Writers: Politics and Pedagogies of Access*. Mahwah, NJ: Erlbaum.

Miller, Carolyn R. 2002. Foreword to *Rhetoric and Kairos: Essays in History, Theory, and Praxis*, edited by Phillip Sipiora and James S. Baumlin, xi–xiii. Albany: SUNY Press.

Miller, Richard E. 2004. "Opinion: Our Future Donors." *College English* 66 (4): 365–79. http://dx.doi.org/10.2307/4140707.

Miller, Richard E. 2005. *Writing at the End of the World*. Pittsburgh: University of Pittsburgh Press.

Morse, Robert. 2010. "Methodology: Undergraduate Ranking Criteria and Weights." *U.S. News and World Report*. August 17. Accessed 8 July 2011. www.usnews.com/education/best-colleges/articles/2013/09/09/best-colleges-ranking-criteria-and-weights.

Mortenson, Thomas G. 2005. "Measurements of Persistence." In *College Student Retention: Formula for Student Success*, edited by Alan Seidman, 31–60. Westport, CT: Praeger.

Obama, Barack Hussein. 2009a. "Address to Joint Session of Congress." *The White House*. February 24. Accessed 8 July 2011. www.whitehouse.gov/the-press-office/Remarks-of-President-Barack-Obama-Address-to-Joint-Session-of-Congress/.

Obama, Barack Hussein. 2009b. "Inaugural Address." *The White House*. January 21. Accessed 8 July 2011. www.whitehouse.gov/blog/inaugural-address/.

Obama, Barack Hussein. 2009c. "Remarks by the President on the American Graduation Initiative." *The White House*. July 14. Accessed 22 July 2011.

www.whitehouse.gov/the_press_office/Remarks-by-the-President-on-the-American-Graduation-Initiative-in-Warren-MI/.

Okun, Morris A., Paul Karoly, Jessica L. Martin, and Annja Benshoff. 2008–2009. "Distinguishing Between Exogenous and Endogenous Intent-to-Transfer Students." *Journal of College Student Retention* 10 (4): 507–24. http://dx.doi.org/10.2190/CS.10.4.f.

O'Toole, Chuck. 2006. "Student Debt: Earnings Premium or Opportunity Cost?" *Connection, New England's Journal of Higher Education* 21 (1): 26. *ProQuest.* Accessed 13 July 2009. www.nebhe.org/info/journal/issues/Connection_Summer06.pdf.

Payne, David. 1989. *Coping with Failure: The Therapeutic Uses of Rhetoric.* Columbia: University of South Carolina Press.

Podis, JoAnne, and Leonard Podis. 2007. "Pedagogical *In Loco Parentis*: Reflecting Power and Parental Authority in the Writing Classroom." *College English* 70 (2): 121–43.

Project on Student Debt. 2010. "Student Debt and the Class of 2009." October. Accessed 8 July 2011. projectonstudentdebt.org/files/pub/classof2009.pdf.

Reichert Powell, Douglas. 2007. *Critical Regionalism: Connecting Politics and Culture in the American Landscape.* Chapel Hill: University of North Carolina Press.

Roemer, Marjorie, Lucille M. Schultz, and Russel K. Durst. 1999. "Reframing the Great Debate on First-Year Writing." *College Composition and Communication* 50 (3): 377–92.

Sallie Mae. 2009. *How Undergraduate Students Use Credit Cards: Sallie Mae's National Study of Usage Rates and Trends 2009.* May. Accessed 27 May 2009. inpathways.net/SLMCreditCardUsageStudy41309FINAL2.pdf.

Sandage, Scott. 2005. *Born Losers: A History of Failure in America.* Cambridge, MA: Harvard University Press.

Scott, Tony. 2005. *Dangerous Writing: Understanding the Political Economy of Composition.* Logan: Utah State University Press.

Seidman, Alan, 2005a. Introduction to *College Student Retention: Formula for Student Success,* edited by Alan Seidman, xi–xiv. Westport, CT: Praeger.

Seidman, Alan, ed. 2005b. "Where We Go from Here: A Retention Formula for Student Success." In *College Student Retention: Formula for Student Success,* edited by Alan Seidman 295–316. Westport, CT: Praeger.

Shor, Ira. 1997. "Our Apartheid: Writing Instruction and Inequality." *Journal of Basic Writing* 16 (1): 91–104.

Sipiora, Phillip. 2002. "Introduction." In *Rhetoric and Kairos: Essays in History, Theory, and Praxis,* edited by Phillip Sipiora and James S. Baumlin, 1–22. Albany, NY: SUNY Press.

Slaughter, Sheila. 2010. "Reflections on Students as Consumers and Students as Captive Markets: Complexities and Contradictions Academic Capitalism." AARE: Australian Association for Research in Education. Accessed 2 August 2010. publications.aare.edu.au/01pap/sla01242.htm.

Slaughter, Sheila, and Larry L. Leslie. 1997. *Academic Capitalism: Politics, Policies, and the Entrepreneurial University.* Baltimore: Johns Hopkins University Press.

Smit, David W. 2004. *The End of Composition Studies.* Carbondale: Southern Illinois University Press.

Smith, Jeff. 1997. "Students' Goals, Gatekeeping, and Some Questions of Ethics." *College English* 59 (3): 299–320. http://dx.doi.org/10.2307/378379.

Smith, John E. 2002. "Time and Qualitative Time." In *Rhetoric and Kairos: Essays in History, Theory, and Praxis*, edited by Phillip Sipiora and James S. Baumlin, 46–57. Albany: SUNY Press.

Soliday, Mary. 2001. "Ideologies of Access and the Politics of Agency." In *Mainstreaming Basic Writers: Politics and Pedagogies of Access*, edited by Gerri McNenny, 55–72. Mahwah, NJ: Erlbaum.

Sommers, Nancy, and Laura Saltz. 2004. "The Novice as Expert: Writing the Freshman Year." *College Composition and Communication* 56 (1): 124–49. http://dx.doi.org/10.2307/4140684.

Sternglass, Marilyn S. 1997. *Time to Know Them: A Longitudinal Study of Writing and Learning at the College Level*. Mahwah, NJ: Erlbaum.

Survey of Student Retention Policies in Higher Education. 2008. New York: Primary Research Group.

Tinto, Vincent. 1987. *Leaving College: Rethinking the Causes and Cures of Student Attrition*. Chicago: University of Chicago Press.

Tinto, Vincent. 2005a. Epilogue to *College Student Retention: Formula for Student Success*, edited by Alan Seidman, 317–33. Westport, CT: Praeger.

Tinto, Vincent. 2005b. Foreword to *College Student Retention: Formula for Student Success*, edited by Alan Seidman, ix–x. Westport, CT: Praeger.

Tinto, Vincent. 2006–2007. "Research and Practice of Student Retention: What Next?" *Journal of College Student Retention* 8 (1): 1–19. http://dx.doi.org/10.2190/4YNU-4TMB-22DJ-AN4W.

Trimbur, John. 2000. "Composition and the Circulation of Writing." *College Composition and Communication* 52 (2): 188–219. http://dx.doi.org/10.2307/358493.

Upcraft, M. Lee, John N. Gardener, and Betsy O. Barefoot, eds. 2005. Introduction to *Challenging and Supporting the First-Year Student: A Handbook for Improving the First Year of College*. San Francisco: Jossey-Bass, a Wiley Imprint.

U.S. Department of Education. 2006. *A Test of Leadership: Charting the Future of U.S. Higher Education*. Washington, DC: U.S. Department of Education. Accessed 27 May 2009. www2.ed.gov/about/bdscomm/list/hiedfuture/reports/final-report.pdf.

Villanueva, Victor. 1993. *Bootstraps: From an American Academic of Color*. Urbana, IL: National Council of Teachers of English.

Wardle, Elizabeth. 2007. "Understanding 'Transfer' from FYC: Preliminary Results of a Longitudinal Study." *WPA: Writing Program Administration* 31 (1/2): 65–85. *Expanded Academic ASAP*. Accessed 31 July 2011. wpacouncil.org/archives/31n1-2/31n1-2wardle.pdf.

Wei, Christina Chang, and Lutz Berkner. 2008. *Trends in Undergraduate Borrowing II: Federal Student Loans in 1995–96, 1999–2000, and 2003–04*. Washington, DC: National Center for Educational Statistics, U.S. Department of Education. Accessed 27 May 2009. nces.ed.gov/pubs2008/2008179rev.pdf.

Weinberg, Daniel H. 2004. "Evidence From Census 2000 About Earnings by Detailed Occupation for Men and Women." *US Census Bureau*. Accessed 27 May 2009. www.census.gov/prod/2004pubs/censr-15.pdf.

Wells, Susan. 1996. "Rogue Cops and Health Care: What Do We Want From Public Writing." *College Composition and Communication* 47 (3): 325–41. http://dx.doi.org/10.2307/358292.

White House 2013. "College Scorecard." Accessed 25 February 2013. http://www.whitehouse.gov/issues/education/higher-education/college-score-card.

Williams, Jeffrey. 2006. "The Pedagogy of Debt." *College Literature* 33 (4): 155–69. http://dx.doi.org/10.1353/lit.2006.0062.

Williams, Raymond. 1983. *Keywords: A Vocabulary of Culture and Society.* New York: Oxford University Press.

Wintre, Maxine Gallandar, Colleen Bowers, Nicole Gordner, and Liora Lange. 2006. "Re-Evaluating the University Attrition Statistic: A Longitudinal Follow-Up Study." *Journal of Adolescent Research* 21 (2): 111–32. http://dx.doi.org/10.1177/0743558405285658.

ABOUT THE AUTHOR

PEGEEN REICHERT POWELL is an associate professor at Columbia College Chicago. Her recent publications include articles about retention in *College Composition and Communication* and *Open Words: Access and English Studies*. She draws regularly on the methodology of critical discourse analysis as demonstrated in pieces recently published in edited collections in the fields of both composition studies and feminist mothering studies. A collection of essays about feminist mothering titled *Mothers Who Deliver: Feminist Interventions in Interpersonal and Public Discourse*, which Pegeen coedited with Jocelyn Fenton Stitt, was published by SUNY Press (2010).

INDEX